THE POWER OF PIVOT

Redefine your limits.
Keep pivoting.
alli Esker

THE POWER OF PIVOT

A FEMALE PERSPECTIVE ON EMBRACING CHANGE

ALLI ESKER

NEW DEGREE PRESS

THE POWER OF PIVOT

A Female Perspective on Embracing Change

ISBN   978-1-64137-904-5 *Paperback*

           978-1-64137-631-0 *Kindle Ebook*

           978-1-64137-633-4 *Ebook*

To my family: Mom, Dad, Ricky, Emmi, and Joey. You are my why.

CONTENTS

———

AUTHOR'S NOTE

———

The year 2020 will without a doubt go down in history as being a pivotal one. As I created and revised my manuscript in the early months of the year, the world came to a screeching halt because of COVID-19.

As it spread, shutting down what felt like everything in its path, I was forced out of my college campus and back into the walls of my childhood home for two months. There, I became aware of a newfound pressure to scrutinize the principles of change that I share with you in the following pages.

Do the principles of being gritty, being innovative, and being vulnerable (just to name a few) truly hold during an event as major as a global health crisis?

Although I was increasingly discouraged by news reports of describing mounting numbers of deaths from the virus, once I dug deeper, I found what I was looking for: radical change and adaptability in the face of mass instability and uncertainty. It will surely be another book for another time, but I discovered female business owners moving entire infrastructures online, local seamstresses sewing masks for our small-town community, and a teary-eyed Peloton instructor expressing her fears and mourning her uncle's death while teaching a cycling class. I read about an elementary school teacher caring for one of her student's newborn baby brother while his family was battling the virus, I saw viral videos of mothers embracing work from home on conference calls while their kids behaved badly in the background, and I learned about entire states allocating resources for women and other marginalized groups to aid in an economic recovery that is equitable for everyone.

For all that the virus has taken from all of us, and will most likely continue to take for an indeterminable length of time into the future, I didn't have to look very far to see *The Power of Pivot* in action on quite possibly the largest scale of my twenty-three years of existence so far.

The answer is yes. I believe these principles endure under every possible circumstance. The principles aren't tethered to a certain environment, but they prevail in the midst of all kinds of environments.

By the end of this book, I hope you will agree.

-Alli

INTRODUCTION

———

"The world as we have created it is a process of our thinking. It cannot be changed without changing our thinking."

-ALBERT EINSTEIN

I've learned that women have a particular power to pivot. Let me show you *why*, and also *how* you can personally experience your own pivots in life more effectively.

My journey towards this realization began on a seemingly ordinary summer day, when I opened my journal and drew out "multiple lives." My pen met the paper, and within a few minutes I produced some measly drawings. I then looked at the three vastly different lives that I had just created. One "life plan" depicted me doing things such as completing a Half Ironman and owning a Tesla. Another, living in a tiny house and managing my own yoga studio. One more depicted me climbing both the corporate American ladder as well as Africa's tallest peak, Mount Kilimanjaro.

As my eyes drew back from each individual life I had just designed, I looked at them in aggregate and realized something fascinating: nothing was *really* stopping me from achieving every single activity and goal I had outlined in all three of the very different lives I had envisioned for myself. But even more interesting, since coming back to these sketches less than a year after creating them, my dreams and goals have changed. I no longer have a burning desire to compete in a Half Ironman, I'm aiming for a full Ironman. Living in a tiny house sounds fun, but perhaps I want to live in a van instead. I think I'd prefer to climb Mount Aconcagua now rather than Kilimanjaro. I realized so many of the things I had drawn out and envisioned myself doing in the future are now no longer relevant. The inspiration of this activity came from the executive director of Stanford's design school, Bill Burnett, who believes there exists many lives to be lived in each and every one of us.[1]

But what does that even mean?

Our brains have this nasty tendency to think of the most obvious answers first. If I had spent more time on my drawings, I probably could have developed close to one hundred lives that I would be wholly satisfied with. Although there isn't anything inherently wrong with arriving at a simple and succinct solution, when it comes to mapping out a life to be lived, I find it much more gratifying and interesting to force myself through various iterations. It helps to open

---

1   Savannah Peterson, "How Many Lives Are You, Really?" *designingyour. life*, July 26, 2016.

up my mind to new possibilities and teaches me to not be afraid of change.

The concept of change can be analyzed from innumerable angles and can be defined in many ways. I'll describe it for you here with a quantitative illustration. In the statistical method of simple linear regression analysis, there's a term known as "ε," or the Greek letter epsilon. For statisticians,"ε," or "error," is meant to describe any part of the data that deviates from the mean, or the average, of the data set. Perhaps you can recall seeing "ε" on display in a graph from a statistics class you've taken, similar to the one below:

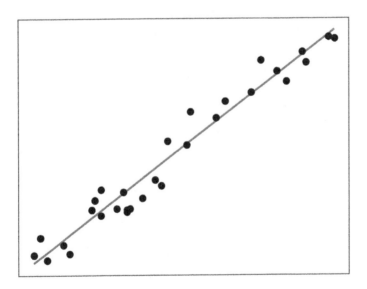

"ε" is a powerful thing. It does the incredible task of capturing the effects of unpredictable random components that exist in the data.[2] In the case of the above graph, "ε" represents all of the dots that don't perfectly fit on the line. In relation to the concept of change, imagine that the line itself represents those things in your life such as your goals and dreams. They provide direction and meaning, propelling you forward on your personal life's mission.

However, "ε" in this case represents the innumerable parts of your life that are changeable, moldable, and adaptable, either by your own conscious doing, or by the environment's doing. "ε" can represent your relationship status, your favorite TV show, or the economy. "ε" guides you in the direction of your goals, but not necessarily perfectly. It could be as simple as, *"What if I turn down this street instead of that one?"* Or as potentially life altering as, *"What if I move to New York instead of Atlanta?"* It's clear that life and the choices we have within it are filled with a lot of "ε." What's compelling about this illustration is that the model of simple linear regression will almost always include some amount of "ε."

This same principle can translate to the human experience at large, as well as women in particular. Think of it this way: As people, we want to minimize error and create a life with choices and adaptions that most closely align with our personal regression line, or in other words, to our goals. However, you can make every effort to control every single variable in your life, perfectly planning and executing every step on the path to your goal, but at the end of the day, as I learned with my drawing activity, the goal itself could change. And then what do you do? When that happens, there's an opportunity

---

2   Asad Ali, "Regression Analysis," *slideshare.net*, December 22, 2013.

to use "ε" to your advantage because within it is the ability to make a conscious pivot for you to create a new regression line that more effectively encapsulates your newly desired goal, ideal, or behavior.

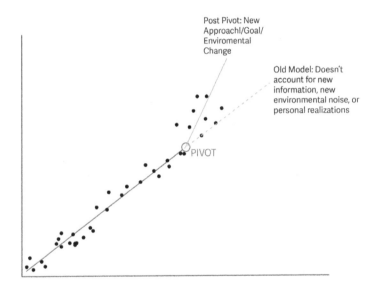

Through my relatively short twenty-three years of existence, I've learned that life is filled with a lot of "ε" and unpredictability. However, I don't think it should be something to be feared, because unpredictability infers that a change of some sort can be made in order to make it more predictable (i.e., a pivot to better fit your new goal or vision). As American philosopher, essayist, and poet Henry David Thoreau put it, "Go confidently in the direction of your dreams! Live the life you've imagined."[3]

---

3   "20 Quotes on Following Your Dreams to Liv. . .ife You've Imagined," *virtuesforlife.com*.

So, what's on your regression line? The line serves as a compass, providing a sense of direction. However, like I've mentioned, very few parts of my life truly fit perfectly into my own model, and I surmise, yours as well. So many things in life are variable. Ask yourself this question to reveal the variability in your life: When was the last time something happened in the exact way you envisioned it?

What I believe is that in the midst of all this "ε" lies opportunity—opportunity to change directions, experience a pivot, and perhaps even live a different life than the one that is perfectly captured by your metaphorical life's regression analysis. We can make every effort to plan our lives out in a certain direction and with particular goals, but ultimately, as ancient Chinese philosopher Lao Tzu says, "If you do not change direction, you may end up where you are heading."[4] There's power in pivoting.

***

I grew up with the belief that my capacity to change, or in other words, experience that point of pivot described above, was dictated by a certain threshold. At a young age, I can vividly recall my mom repeating the Tony Robbins quote, "Change happens when the pain of staying the same is greater than the pain of change."[5]

What is Robbins really saying?

---

4 "INSPIRING QUOTES BY LAO TZU," *optimize.me.*

5 Paul Heagen, "The Pain of Change Is Not Going to Change Anything," *definingmoments.me*, May 23, 2016.

Imagine a Minnesotan lake in January. At one point, the lake will freeze. From a chemist's perspective, the two variables that dictate the phase change of the water from liquid to solid are: 1. air pressure and 2. temperature. Once the temperature becomes low enough or the pressure becomes high enough, or a certain mix of these two variables is achieved, the threshold for freezing is reached, and the liquid will become solid.

Applying the same idea as Robbins, the two variables required to exceed some threshold catalyzing change are: 1. the level of pain and 2. the frequency of the event. This theory surmises that if we experience low levels of pain infrequently, then we have very little incentive to change physically, behaviorally, emotionally, or socially.

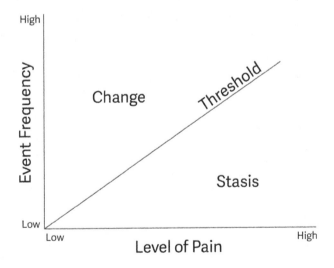

If we experience a high level of pain infrequently, we could also still lie below the critical threshold. Many of us know the physical pain of stepping on a Lego (and if you don't, you're lucky).

While the pain is rather excruciating, this one-time event, as far as the Robbins-esque view goes, is probably not enough pain to cause you to make some kind of sustainable lifestyle change, which in this case, would be picking up the Lego.

However, if the frequency increases, such as, say, you step on a Lego for ten consecutive days in a row, the threshold would be exceeded and you would be inspired to change (i.e., clean up the Legos!). Similarly, any event with a low level of pain but comparatively higher level of frequency would also exceed the critical threshold and thus, you would experience a change.

Events with high levels of pain and high frequency speak for themselves. Imagine walking over a bed of hot coals. Every step is unbearably painful, and you seek relief with each step you take. On the very first step, you would exceed the critical threshold, driving you to change your behavior (i.e., jump off the bed of coals or start running through them to escape the pain).

The Robbins theory to change argues that only those events in which we experience *enough* pain and with *enough* frequency propel people to pivot from their current state into a new one.

Do women really behave like this?

When I set out to write this book, I wanted to put this theory to the test and see whether or not it held true. Is pain really the best way to describe why women change? I scrutinized this theory, analyzing if it really was the best way to describe all the diverse ways in which women create change.

The "draw your life" activity I completed facilitated my discovery of the realization that at any one moment, even if I may want one thing, I still often find myself desiring something different at different times, for a multitude of reasons. Additionally, every so often, the environment in which I'm functioning changes, as I've described with the regression analysis metaphor. This environmental change in itself facilitates a change of my own expectations. My ability to change is a function of a multitude of internal and external factors. I've experienced many psychological, emotional, and cultural-based explanations to this phenomenon, (which we'll dig into throughout this book), but for now, the more fundamental question I seek to answer is:

"What drives me, and women in general, to change?"

I've learned that so many variables beyond pain facilitate change. From what I've uncovered, pain doesn't appear to be one of the requirements for women to change, even in places where pain is inescapable. For example, in the world of ultra-marathons, a common question is, "What's your demon?" The subtext of this question is, "What makes you put yourself through such pain and suffering?"

Courtney Dauwalter, one of the world's best-known ultra-marathoners, doesn't seem to be suppressed by any kind of pain threshold. She has most notably won the Moab 240, a 240-mile race, beating the second-place finisher by over ten hours. One interviewer describes her saying, "When you talk to her, she seems so normal, there's no demon there. I'm like, waiting to meet a demon. You know, I'm like, 'Where's your demon?' 'How are you getting through that?' Her demons are quiet demons. It's there. It has to be. . ."

Dauwalter responds to the interviewer, in her typical smiling and jovial manner and says, "Everybody's got a demon. I don't know that I have a demon. I think, I don't like to fail, and I want to finish everything that I start. Is that a demon?"[6] It appears that for Dauwalter, a *focus on achieving,* rather than an escape from some kind of pain, is what propels her forward to change. Of course, as her exhausted legs reach well over mile one hundred during her races, pain, at least the kind that's physical in nature, certainly plays a major role. But in Dauwalter's case, she transcends it.

Or take three-time record holder Fiona Oakes as another example. She's the fastest woman in aggregate time to complete a marathon on each continent, but ironically, running isn't her passion. She's a vegan and sustainability advocate who uses her platform to raise awareness for the cause of environmentalism. Her passion for the cause is what motivates her mile after mile.

After completing the Marathon Des Sables, a grueling 250km (that's about six marathons in a row) through the scorching hot Moroccan Sahara, she stoically says, "It's do something else now. Go home, feed my lambs. That's where I want to be. That's where I so want to be."[7] For Oakes, it's an outward *focus on the world at large* that drives her forward.

---

6   Dream Lens Media, ""Courtney Dewaulter," April 2, 2019, video, 38:52.

7   First Spark Media, "Running for Good" 2018, video, 1:14:11.

Although most of us aren't elite athletes, the lesson here for each of us is that these women have self-elected to enter painful situations, and instead of escaping the pain, they choose to accept it and move forward step by step within it. Courtney and Fiona are embracing pain so they can reach their goals. They are literally moving through the "hot bed of coals" as slowly as possible, either for the sake of the experience itself or to achieve some higher purpose.

If we are to believe Robbins theory of change, in this example, from a physical standpoint, stopping at mile eighty of a one-hundred-mile race would be less painful than continuing on to mile one hundred. What makes these two women continue to dive into the deepest parts of the "pain cave" instead of aligning to Robbins' theory and changing from their current state of running (by quitting) when the pain of continuing (staying the same) is much greater? Pain isn't the instigator of change in this case.

What kind of model would these women best fit into?

From what I've learned personally, and from the stories of the women I've researched and talked to, Robbins' theory of transformation is not exhaustive in its application to the concept of change.

From a personal account, I've always been fascinated with my own capacity to adapt, pivot, and change when faced with challenges, but also in events and circumstances that weren't specifically arduous or painful. I took on the project of writing this very book because I was curious. From my stasis of not being a writer to the transformation of being a published author, there was no pain involved to push me toward achieving this goal and actualizing this pivot. I hope you can think of several pivotal points in your own life that weren't the result of some kind of painful external stimuli that inspired your change.

Throughout the process of writing this book, I had conversations with many women from all walks of life about their personal journeys, struggles, and pivotal moments. I sought to explore what is at the root of their life's evolutions and pivots. Through this journey I discovered that the Tony Robbins quote doesn't quite capture the true essence of change. Most all of my life's pivotal moments, and the stories of pivotal moments in the lives of the women I've talked to and researched, do not align with this theory of transformation. Our ability to change is not a product of the pain we experience or the frequency at which we experience it. Pain is not the only variable—and not even a significant one at that—capable of pushing women to pivot.

I believe that a single Lego can change your life.

Change doesn't have to be necessitated by some big painful event or many small consecutive painful events. It can happen from things that are simple in nature, and even pain-free. I've created my own framework to describe the pivots we can experience throughout life. The important thing here is that this framework *includes* the theory that small-in-magnitude, even pain-free, events and circumstances can be the catalyst to someone's lasting change *just as much* as a large, painful event can be.

	Negative	Positive
Large	Life-Threatening	Lottery
Small	Lego	Lollipop

We've talked about the "Lego" moments as imbedded in Robbins' theory: those inconvenient, annoying occurrences you may face on a day-to-day basis. The "Lollipop" quadrant is also a small-scale circumstance, but a positive one. I've named this quadrant after a TED Talk from Drew Dudley called "Leading with Lollipops." Dudley says, "I worry sometimes that we spend so much time celebrating amazing things that hardly anybody can do, that we convinced ourselves that those are the only things worth celebrating." He goes on to tell a story of a time he handed out lollipops at his university and how that small interaction helped a freshman student decide she wasn't going to drop out. The funny thing is, when she thanked him years later, he had no recollection of that specific encounter.[8] The lollipop quadrant represents anything in our lives that is generally pleasant, or even serendipitous, that we might encounter. Someone at the

---

8   TEDx Talks, "TEDxToronto—Drew Dudley "Leading with Lollipops," October 7, 2010, video, 6:20.

drive-thru in the car in front of you paying for your coffee could be a lollipop moment.

Let's move diagonally to "Life-Threatening." The name was inspired by our biological tendencies as human beings. When we are under extreme stress, anxiety, or trauma, our brains start to do a lot of weird things. The amygdala, also known as the fear center of the brain, lights up, and sends signals to our body to push blood to our extremities, activating our fight or flight response. This reaction was great for our ancestors when we were fighting saber-toothed tigers, but it's not so healthy for us today when most events we face aren't actually life-threatening. This quadrant, as depicted, holds all changes driven by large-in-magnitude and negative-in-direction events, whether they are actually life-threatening or not.

The last is "Lottery." These are the large and positive events we experience. Your wedding, your promotion, or your travel adventures—this quadrant encompasses all of those things we'd label as "the best moments in our lives." They are rather self-evident.

To summarize my theory: Whether the catalyst is negative or positive, large or small, each quadrant in the framework includes something that could drive us to change, and in total, all boxes are collectively exhaustive to include all of life's moments that propel us to change. I'll be coming back to this framework throughout each chapter as a tool for explaining the types of changes experienced within the stories of the women I've researched and spoken to.

***

Why attempt to explore a female-centric view of change?

I chose to explore women's stories for both strategic and personal reasons. For me, the stories that inspire me the most come from the vast pool of women on this earth that are doing incredible things. When I picture myself accomplishing some monumental task, I imagine all of the women who've come before me. I imagine Kristin Fleschner, who never uses her blindness as an excuse, or Gitanjali Rao, who had to convince researchers and scientists that she "wasn't just a kid trying to do experiments", or even Polina Marinova, who fiercely and passionately isn't afraid to ask "stupid" questions. By thinking about these women, (all of whom you'll learn more about in the following chapters) and other women like them, I can't help but be inspired by their impact on this world and feel intrinsically compelled to democratize their stories through this book.

Although the "Female Condition" exists (as we'll learn about in Chapter 1), women have specific advantages that they can develop if they choose, that can aide in their ability to pivot personally and more effectively deal with environmental changes around them. I call this ability "The Female Advantage." In the following chapters, I'll use the stories of women to illustrate the powerful principles of this Female Advantage so you can start recognizing them and applying them in your own life. You'll learn that underlying a woman's ability to change and adapt are many principles such as being gritty, innovative, vulnerable, and unafraid to ask questions. The stories you read will exemplify each of those principles along with the principles of avoiding the victim mentality, believing in yourself, cultivating gratitude, and defining success in your own way.

You're the perfect reader for this book if you're looking for a fresh take on the concept of change. You value the female perspective and want to learn from other people with views and ideas different from your own. As a reader, my goal for you is two-fold in nature: to learn something new and be inspired. I urge you to break apart the stories that I share and discover how different situations and circumstances fit into the framework that I've built. Be curious and play around with this framework in your own life. See if it holds true for you. Discover how small or large, negative or positive events have spurred change for you personally and in the women whose stories are featured in this book. The stories in these pages are real, raw, and vulnerable. They cover a multitude of topics from business and entrepreneurship to trauma and loss. You will learn from these women's conscious decisions to pivot, transform, and make an impact in the world.

My ultimate hope is that you are encouraged to look inside yourself—realizing, reawakening, or reaffirming your own ability to change in any way you can dream. Let's pivot.

CHAPTER 1

HOW WE GOT HERE: A BRIEF HISTORY OF WOMEN

How wonderful it is that nobody need wait a single moment before starting to change the world.

-ANNE FRANK

Ursula is not the antagonist.

What?

Well, she wasn't *supposed* to be the antagonist. In the early 1800s, when Hans Christian Anderson dipped his pen into his inkwell, both Ursula (her name at the time simply being "sea-witch") and the original story of *The Little Mermaid* were born. But, when Ursula was originally created, she wasn't the villainous half-human, half-octopus creature that we know today from the eponymous Disney childhood favorite movie.

In the original story, Hans created the sea witch as a neutral enabler. After saving the handsome prince in a shipwreck, all the Little Mermaid desired was to reconnect with him so that he might fall in love with her. Seeking advice, she decided to go to the sea witch, and as the story goes, she believed that the sea witch could, "Perhaps advise and help me!" The sea witch provided her precisely the assistance she was seeking: a special drink that would transform her mermaid tail into a pair of legs.[9]

So why did Disney villainize an originally neutral character?

This isn't a novel concept. As 19th century English politician and poet Lord Byron echoes, "The best prophet of the future is the past."[10] History seems to always have a way of replaying past storylines in the present, and the application of this idea is easily demonstrated in the stories and stereotypes of women. The stories throughout the past few thousand years that depict a female character as villainous are prolific. Whether it be Cruella de Ville in *The Hundred and One Dalmatians* or Mrs. Bennet in Jane Austen's *Pride and Prejudice*, an antagonist is almost a baseline requirement for any good story.

So then, it makes sense that the directors and screenwriters of the *Little Mermaid* movie saw an opportunity to build a more compelling storyline by defiling the original character Hans had created. It also happens to be the reality that a female villain, in Disney's case, is a tried and true method for

---

9 Hans Christian Anderson, *The Little Mermaid*, Hans Christian Andersen Centre at the University of Southern Denmark, 2014.

10 "George Byron Quotes," *allauthor.com*.

creating stimulating storylines and box office hits. However, it's not only Disney that utilizes overarching storylines of stereotypical feminine weaknesses as a way to elevate some kind of agenda (in this case, profit). Let's dig a little deeper into the historical context of how women have been represented across cultures and societies throughout the last few millennia. But first, let's examine the overarching idea of "The Human Condition" before we dive deeper.

Women have biological and psychological traits that differ from our male counterparts. Does this mean that our stories are different? It appears that way. However, you'll soon discover that regardless of gender, the stories observed throughout history and through the lens of the women researched and interviewed in this book all embody universal themes we can all relate to such as failure, loss, rejection, overcoming, achieving, and winning.

Although these themes are expressed differently by whoever is experiencing them, it's in these universal ideals that humanity is tied together as a whole. Without the existence of overarching stories and collective themes imbedded throughout the human experience, we wouldn't be where we are today. Hellen Keller puts it this way: "Alone we can do so little; together we can do so much."[11]

And turns out, we have done a lot so far as humans. If Earth's history was condensed into one twenty-four-hour period, modern humans wouldn't appear until 11:59:59 p.m. In that

---

11 Samantha DiFeliciantonia, "Alone we can do so little; together we can do so much." Helen Keller, *teambonding.com*.

metaphorical one second of modern human existence, we've managed to migrate out of Africa, develop complex languages, make the move from hunting and gathering to agriculture, build the Great Pyramids of Giza, develop what are now modern-day institutions, and most importantly, invent the iPhone.[12]

However, throughout our relatively short existence as rulers of this world, which includes the development of many incredible innovations and ideas, we've had numerous drawbacks and struggles, many of which were brought on by our own complex decision-making behavior as a self-declared intelligent species. Historically, we've participated in child sacrifice, eliminated entire people groups via the transmission of disease and violent encounters, waged wars over plots of land simply for their religious utility, and pumped trillions of pounds of greenhouse gases into our air. Unfortunately, those are just some of many of the atrocities humankind has committed throughout our existence.

It's easy to say, "Well that's not me. I didn't participate in the Holocaust or fight in the American-Indian war." No, you didn't. But the repetition of this insidious behavior across geographies and history points to something deep inside each of us: a duality of both good and evil. Philosopher Arthur Schopenhauer summarizes it nicely: "Man is the only animal which causes pain to others with no other object than causing pain. . . No animal ever torments another for the sake of tormenting: but man does so, and it is this which constitutes the

---

12   Tim Urban, Putting Time in Perspective—UPDATED, *waitbutwhy.com*, August 22, 2013.

diabolical nature which is far worse than the merely bestial."[13] Although we as humans have done countless amazing things, it doesn't take a meticulous combing through of history to distinguish the injustices we've imposed on ourselves and our world at large.

What about the "Female Condition?"

With the Human Condition considered, let's explore the smaller sect within it that hasn't been fleshed out completely quite yet: The Female Condition. I'll define it as the specific, female-centric struggles that women have experienced throughout history up until this very moment. Women have been undervalued, misidentified, exploited, objectified, blamed, and ostracized for thousands of years.

With an economic lens, let's travel back about twelve thousand years to when the Neolithic Revolution began. This era serves as a point in time where humanity began turning away from an equality-driven social system to one of patriarchy. As anthropologists discovered, before the Neolithic Revolution, both men and women were taking part in hunting, gathering, and toolmaking. However, when our ancestors made the transition to farming, surpluses of food and other goods developed, creating less of an incentive for everyone to take part in subsistence roles. With the principle of comparative advantage in mind, it was the men who took part in the heavy lifting, labor intensive duties. This left women to their comparative advantage of tending to children and

---

13 Arthur Schopenhauer, THE ESSAYS OF ARTHUR SCHOPENHAUER, gutenberg.org, January 18, 2004.

taking part in more domestic duties. Although the concepts of labor and caretaking have evolved greatly, this condition still prevails, at least in some capacity, even today.[14]

From a biological view, researchers at the Sapienza University of Rome sought to study the impact of agriculture on the emergence of patriarchy. By studying the DNA and genetic makeup of forty populations in sub-Saharan Africa today, the researchers found evidence that women in hunter-gatherer societies were more likely to remain with their mothers after marriage than women from agricultural societies. The reverse was true for men, which suggests that agriculture is correlated with patriarchal societies. What archaeologists and scientists uncovered during the time period of the Neolithic Revolution is a pivot: a move from an egalitarian societal system to one of patriarchy. Anthropologist Amy Parish reminds us that, "It's tempting to assume male dominance is the natural state of human society. It isn't." [15]

We see that women's roles in society have been molded over thousands and thousands of years. The move from hunting and gathering to agriculture appears to have significantly impacted the roles of males and females due primarily to the simple but powerful principle of comparative advantage. For these early societies, it's possible that many women's talents and abilities to contribute to society in more atypical ways were squelched because they were inherently undervalued

---

14 John Zerzan, "Patriarchy, Civilization, and the Origins of Gender," *theanarchistlibrary.org*, April 13, 2010.

15 Anil Ananthaswam. . .ate Douglas, "The origins of sexism: How men came to rule 12,000 years ago," *newscientist.com*, April 18, 2018.

from the start, which forced them into more stereotypical roles.

Keeping with the historical perspective of The Female Condition, we can find many ancient texts and art forms emphasizing a woman's physical attributes, such as her sexual fertility and feminine figure. For example, the ancient Egyptians had a goddess of infertility, Nephthys, who was depicted as a vulture and non-coincidently also served as the goddess of funerals. Even one of the earliest Vedic texts in the Indian culture reads, "O woe is the woman who does not carry out the provided role of a mother [birth of sons]. O woe the unmarried, woe the childless, woe the mother of daughters, the widow." Women who were unable to get pregnant were viewed as possessed by Nirrti, a ferocious goddess.[16] Ironically enough, for all of the positive value placed on a woman's appearance and physical reproductive abilities that exists throughout history and today, many examples of the negative value placed around these ideals is not hard to come by.

The Aphrodite sculpture, created circa 100 B.C., on display in the Louvre in Paris is a fitting example of this ideal. Half-nakedly draped in a toga, she perfectly embodies the ideals of fertility and sensuality.[17] Although not necessarily inaccurate, as females are endowed with the ability to bear children of course, it is the illumination of these themes that have led to the exploitation and objectification of her body

---

16 JR Thorpe "How Infertility Was Talked About Throughout History—Because to Figh. . .aboo, You Need To Understand Its Origins," *bustle. com*, April 14, 2015.

17 Marie-Bénédicte Astier, Aphrodite, known as the "Venus de Milo," louvre. fr.

and physical capabilities for thousands of years. This logic undermines a woman's ability to contribute to society beyond her reproductive or child-rearing abilities, contributing to a wrongful conflation of what society assumes women are capable of opposed to what they truly are capable of.

Unfortunately, this misidentification has even led to the mass exploitation of women today. Research at the American Psychological Association found that girls in media are depicted in a sexual manner more often than boys.[18] In one study on print media by Wesleyan University, it was found that, of advertisements that featured women, over 50 percent were portrayed in a sexual way.[19]

Even more, UNICEF reports that, "Approximately fifteen million adolescents between the ages of fifteen and nineteen have experienced forced sexual intercourse or sexual acts at some point in their lives," and, "In the United States, 18 percent of girls report that by age seventeen they have been victims of a sexual assault or abuse at the hands of another adolescent."[20] History repeats itself once again, as we see today that the value society places on the female body actually seems to be counterproductive. Even more, the effects of physical objectification across cultures and societies has deeply imbedded psychological implications, where, according to the Dove Self Esteem Project, only 11 percent

18   "Report of the APA Task Force on the Sexualization of Girls," *American Psychological Association*, 2007.

19   Julie M. Stankiewic. . .rancine Rosselli, "Women as Sex Objects and Victims in Print Advertisements," *Springer Scienc. . .usiness Media*, January 15, 2008.

20   Jaimee Swif. . .annah Gould, "Not an Object: On Sexualization and Exploitation of Women and Girls," *unicefusa.org*, January 15, 2020.

of girls worldwide would call themselves beautiful. The clear exploitation of women remains a problem and has plagued the female condition for many millennia.

From an individual account, I can vividly recall many times during my childhood when I personally experienced the value that society placed on the female body and women's physical appearance.

My older sister Emmi was, and still is, always more outgoing and charismatic than me. At the park or at our brothers' baseball games growing up, she'd always manage to win over crowds of other children and inspire them to follow her as their rightful leader, whether that be to the concession stand for snacks or a stream nearby in the woods. She'd single-handedly orchestrate complex games that somehow made everyone feel included and valued. She had a way of winning people over and garnering much attention from her tribe of loyal disciples to build her empire.

These children loved her. I recall all of the attention and compliments she'd receive from the other kids we'd just met minutes before:

"You're so pretty."

"Your shirt is sooooooo cute!"

"I just love your hair!"

This pattern began occurring when I was seven or so and serves as one of the first instances in which I learned just how much society values a woman's physical appearance. Although I would take part in the games, I recall feeling excluded and undervalued because I wasn't receiving the same attention as Emmi. *Why do they all like her more than me?* I yearned for compliments on my appearance and concluded at quite a young age that if I wasn't receiving them, the logical assumption would be that—just like the 89 percent of girls in the Dove study believed—I simply wasn't beautiful.

Looking back, this story is a bit trite, but in the moment, little Alli was genuinely confused and hurt when this story kept repeating itself throughout my childhood. This example serves to exemplify the expectations that societies bestow on the female demographic and how they personally impact each of us, even at a very young age.

***

Other than her appearance and physical abilities, we can further explore other ways women have been portrayed throughout history. Women have been depicted as mass manipulators and temptresses in many works of literature and ancient texts. The Genesis creation story can be interpreted (albeit I'd say incorrectly so) to depict Eve as being a temptress and the one who brings evil unto man via her disobedience of God's command to not eat the fruit of the tree of knowledge of good and evil. Even the name Eve itself can be translated as "snake" in Hebrew.

Many other creation stories depict women in similar lights. Take the ancient Greeks' creation story for example. It depicts Pandora, one of the first women, as being plagued by intense curiosity to open a box that Zeus explicitly instructed her not to. As the story goes, she opens it, and what came out were all of the plagues of this world: sickness, pain, envy, and greed. From an ancient literary view, we can see how women have received a bulk of the blame across various mediums.[21]

Even today, the depiction of the woman as some kind of seducer, temptress, and evil being is evident. As we've already seen, Walt Disney leaned heavily on this theme in many of his works. The childhood classic *Sleeping Beauty* includes the witch Maleficent, who, due to her jealousy of Princess Aurora's beauty, declared: "The princess shall indeed grow in grace and beauty, beloved by all who know her. But . . . before the sun sets on her sixteenth birthday, she shall prick her finger on the spindle of a spinning wheel—and die!"

Or take *Snow White*, where the Evil Queen tries to kill the eponymous protagonist with a poisoned apple. In her own words, the Evil Queen instructs the huntsman to "Take her far into the forest. Find some secluded glade where she can pick wildflowers [and] . . . kill her!" And going back to *The Little Mermaid*, in the song *Poor Unfortunate Souls*, Ursula sings, "I admit that in the past I've been a nasty. They weren't kidding when they called me, well, a witch." She lives up to that nomenclature, transforming into a beautiful woman and manipulating (however unsuccessfully so) Prince Eric into marrying her.[22]

---

21 "Greek Creation Myth," *cs.williams.edu*.

22 Sejal Kapadia Pocha, "The 25 greatest female villains in film," *stylist.co.uk*, 2014.

Other than the fact that Disney heavily relies on these stereotypical evil elements of the female persona, there's another fascinating pattern that arises: Although most women can't relate to an evil queen trying to poison her with an apple, or even the other stories for that matter, today, what she can relate to is the idea of facing some kind of force that is against her on a daily basis. In the case of Disney, all of these stories depict a young, seemingly innocent and beautiful female protagonist facing an older, less attractive female antagonist.

This doesn't seem to be a coincidence, as research from the University of Arizona found that women are ruder to each other compared to men and meaner than men to women. With regard to ageism, in a professional setting, it's also not uncommon for an older, more seasoned women to be intimidated by a younger woman. *What if she is chosen over me for a promotion we are both seeking?*[23] One does not have to look far to see that this pattern does not just occur in our favorite Disney movies. This pattern is reality today.

Along the same vein, further research reveals that women in the workplace face more incivility from both men and women for not adhering to gender norms than their male counterparts who do the same. This points to an uphill battle for women specifically, who may be facing both male and female real-life antagonists. Comparatively, men display less incivility toward women than women do amongst themselves.[24]

---

23 Katerina Ang, "Why women are meaner to each other than men are to women," *marketwatch.com*, March 5, 2018.

24 Allison S. Gabriel, Marcus M. Butt. . .ichael T. Sliter, "Women Experience More Incivility at Work—Especially from Other Women," *hbr.org*, March 28, 2018.

Professional tennis player Serena Williams provides a thoughtful reminder for all women when she says, "The success of every woman should be the inspiration of another. We should raise each other up."[25] And first female US Secretary of State Madeleine Albright is a bit more candid when she says, "There is a special place in hell for women who do not help other women."[26] In a world where incivility or injustice is a prevalent experience for almost all women, it's important for each of us to ask ourselves what role we are playing to bring equity and equality to all.

We've explored the concepts of being undervalued, misidentified, blamed, and objectified as part of The Female Condition. Ostracization also plays a role in The Female Condition throughout history to present times. As institutions developed and modern societies arose, women were not granted certain rights, whether they were social, political, or professional. Even one of the most biologically healthy and natural occurrences, menstruation, has hindered women for thousands of years. It's so very ironic that those same ancient societies that worshipped a woman's fertility shunned her for her menstruation.

The changes undergone by the female body during puberty are quite extraordinary, yet even today, it's also quite taboo. In Bill Bryson's book *The Body*, he shares that, "Perhaps nothing says more about our delicacy toward matter genital than the word 'pudendum'—meaning the external genitals,

---

25 Tanvi Dubey, "10 inspirational quotes by Serena Williams that show what it takes to b...hampion," *yourstory.com*, September 26, 2019.

26 Madeleine Albright, "Madeleine Albright: My Undiplomatic Moment," *nytimes.com*, February 12, 2016.

particularly those of a woman—comes from the Latin word for 'to be ashamed.'"[27]

The concept of the female body, and particularly menstruation preventing women from having basic societal rights, was seen as something to be ashamed of, not only in ancient societies, but even today. Take a few present-day developing countries as a case study. Many girls, for a variety of reasons, are forced to miss school when they are menstruating. A 2016 study conducted by Human Rights Watch found that one in ten girls misses school because of menstruation. Another survey conducted in Bangladesh found that 41 percent of girls ages eleven to seventeen missed three days of school every month due to improper sanitary care.[28]

These studies only looked at the educational deficiencies that young girls faced as a result of menstruation. Now, imagine what the psychological and emotional implications could be. Even in the United States today, the concept of menstruation is still taboo. A quick qualitative survey from some close friends reveals quite a lot.

One described it this way: "The first time I got my period, I felt scared." Another friend says she was embarrassed, while another recalls the humiliation of having to connect with her aunts, uncles, and cousins on Facetime to share the news. One more remembers kindly asking her parents to not throw a party for the occasion.

---

27 Bill Bryson, *The Body. . .uide for Participants,* (New York: Penguin Random House, 2019).

28 "One in ten girls in sub-Saharan Africa miss school during their period," gemreportunesco.com, April 24, 2018.

It seems like it's almost universal in nature to associate having a developed female body and a first period with at least some level of shame, like the word "pudendum" that Bryson referenced. Unfortunately, this natural bodily process continues to not only shame women today but hinders her capacity to succeed, or to simply be a functional member of society, across the globe.

And then there's yet another taboo worth exploring: Politics. The political realm seems to be one of the most untapped and slow-to-mature establishments for women to achieve equality historically. Take ancient China for example. Even on the most fundamental basis, it was widely accepted that it was better to be born a man than a woman. This belief lives in the laws written at the time. In the Chinese legal system, a man could divorce his wife for a plethora of reasons, whether that be her failure to bear a son, her affliction with a disease, or even her tendency to talk too much. On what grounds could a woman divorce her husband? Only if he mistreated her family. According to the principles of "Confucian Law," women were accepted as inferior beings.

Ancient Athens excluded women from courts and assemblies and legally prohibited them from taking part in contracts worth any significant amount of money. Respectable women were assumed to not even appear in public whatsoever. Participation in the government was completely closed off to women. Both women and slaves lived under the total control of the male head of household. Similarly, the ancient Romans held the principle "pater familias," where, the male head of household would exercise absolute authority over his wife and children. Women couldn't vote, hold public office, or serve in the military in any capacity.[29]As we see, the thread of The Female Condition is profuse in almost every historical political institution.

But what has the landscape of politics, law, and government been like in modern times for women? Early America adopted English Common Law, an Anglo-Saxon and Norman-inspired code of conduct that suspended women's rights in marriage with the belief that the man and woman become one in the same. In 1777, all states passed laws to limit women's right to vote. It wasn't until 1839 that the first state, Mississippi, legally allowed women the right to own property. Over fifty years later, Wyoming was the first state that allowed women the right to vote. It would be thirty more years, in 1920, when the Nineteenth Amendment would guarantee women voting rights in the United States.[30]

A few countries only recently allowed women to have voting rights, such as Saudi Arabia in 2015. Saudi women were also just recently allowed access to healthcare and education without consent from a guardian such as a father, brother, or husband. In modern Afghanistan in 2014, women faced threats from the Taliban when they flooded to voting booths or ran for office. Although not legally barred from voting, in Kenya many women are discouraged from walking long distances, which keeps them away

---

29 Ashley Cowie, "Ancient Laws and Women's Rights: The 6000-Year-Old World War Continues," *ancient-origins.net*, November 12, 2018.

30 "Timeline of Legal History of Women in the United States," *nationalwomenshistoryalliance.org*.

from voting booths. More so, pregnant women in Western Kenya aren't allowed to be seen in public, thus also losing their right to vote.[31]

In the political realm, voting is a tangible metric for guaranteeing that a woman's voice is heard and that her ideas and insights are valued. To withhold voting rights to women implies that they are not equally valued in society. Wangari Maathai, Kenyan parliament member and the first African woman to win the Nobel Peace Prize, emphasized this ideal when she said, "Human rights are not things you put on the table for people to enjoy. These are things you fight for and then protect."[32]

As we've uncovered through a multitude of instances and examples, a woman is bound in many ways by The Female Condition. What makes the overarching issue of equality even more convoluted is that, as we've seen, the issue of inequality has been embedded in our culture and society from the beginning of civilization. The systemic nature and profuse spread of this problem makes proposing a solution to this issue difficult. It appears to be a topic that is so much more than an external issue, and could very well be perceived as a fundamental psychological flaw in humanity at large.

How then, is it possible to change humanity's views on equality?

---

31 Georgia Aspinall, "Here Are the Countries Where It's Still Really Difficult for Women to Vote," *graziadaily.co.uk*, June 2, 2018.

32 "Secretary-General's remarks to General Assembly on Human Rights Defenders [as delivered]," *un.org*, December 18, 2018.

This is an incredibly complicated problem, and I have no singular solution (or any solution at all for that matter). However, some good news I can share is that, over the past hundred years or so, the world at large has seen a positive change toward more egalitarian ideologies and beliefs.

Recall that women began as equal to men as hunters and gatherers tens of thousands of years ago—only later succumbing to the institutions of oppression and inferior social expectations as expressed by The Female Condition—but have now more recently made much progress in terms of establishing their identities and place in society. Nonetheless, the root issue of inequality is conceived by human bias and nurtured by the systems in which those ideas and values function within.

Even with what appears to be a more equal world today than even a few hundred years ago, because of one's cultural upbringing and the existence of stereotypical gender roles being depicted in media, among a multitude of other factors, everyone and every organization is bound to some level of predeterminism. A simple question one can ask to test this stereotypical tendency in each of us is to ask yourself, "When you think of female roles what do you think of? And when you think of male roles, what do you think of?" The answers to these questions reveal the inclination of humans to undermine a woman's true potential from the start. Try administering this riddle to some friends or family, and I surmise you'll see the deeply imbedded beliefs of gender roles evidently.

A father and son get in a car crash and are rushed to the hospital. The father dies. The boy is taken to the operating room and the surgeon says, "I can't operate on this boy, because he's my son." How is this possible?[33]

This isn't supposed to be a brain teaser, yet you'll find many people unable to figure out that one very rational possibility is that the doctor is the boy's mother. This is, in part, due to the inherent bias of associating the word "doctor" with "male." But of course, we could flip it the other way too. When you think of "babysitter," you probably envision a female caregiver. Although these associations in and of themselves aren't inherently bad because well, it is factual that there are more male surgeons in the world than female surgeons and more female babysitters in the world than male babysitters. But they point to the deeply held beliefs we have about both men and women and their place in society, and under these beliefs exist self-imposed limitations for all.

***

We've rumbled through the concept of the human condition and parsed out various factors affecting the state of The Female Condition apparent throughout history and up until today. It might have all sounded like a dump of bad news, but like I alluded to above, there has been a more recent shift, and I have some compelling insights still left to share with you.

---

33   Chris McCarthy, "English Riddle: Can you answer the question?," *ecenglish.com*, November 16, 2008.

As we've seen in the examples of ancient China, Rome, and Greece, history has no shortage of examples of patriarchal societies, yet there are several instances of egalitarian and matriarchal societies that have existed and flourished in the past. Take the Navajo Native American tribe for example. From the 1600s to the 1800s, research suggests that its tribal system was particularly equal in terms of gender, especially from an economic standpoint. Both men and women cared for the livestock, and women added value to the tribe through the creation of pottery and baskets. In the Navajo tribe, inheritance was usually distributed equally among children, and both husband and wife could initiate divorce. Additionally, mothers and grandmothers were leaders of clans and generally had the final word on family matters.[34]

From a political lens, not all ancient political systems were inherently anti-woman. Ancient Egypt, one of the greatest civilizations to have ever existed, had a legal code that gave women the same rights as men, allowing them to own property and slaves, represent themselves in judicial affairs, and divorce their husband if they wished. Egyptologist Barbara Watterson says an ancient Egyptian's rights "depended upon her social class, not her sex."[35]

I want to encourage you that what we see throughout history is not a conclusive pattern of inequality across all societies. We can begin to examine how women have been valued in

---

34   Holly Kearl, "Elusive Matriarchy: The Impact of the Native American and Feminist Movements on Navajo Gender Dynamics," *Santa Clara University Undergraduate Journal of History, Series II*, 2006.

35   Joshua J. Mark, "Women in Ancient Egypt," *ancient.eu*, November 4, 2016.

the past and have added value in the communities they functioned within. Perhaps there's an advantage for societies and institutions that view women as equal and able.

From a modern perspective, Harvard Business Review released an article titled "Research: Women Score Higher Than Men in Most Leadership Skills" in 2019. According to an analysis on thousands of 360-degree reviews, women at various companies in management positions outscored men on seventeen of the nineteen metrics used in the study. Some of the highest-rated capability measures that women excelled in were taking initiative, practicing resilience, and practicing self-development.[36]

Another study administered to US adults in 2018 found women in top executive positions to be comparatively better than men at things like "creating a safe and respectful workplace" and "valuing people from different backgrounds." However, women ranked worse than men on the metric of "negotiating profitable deals" and "being willing to take risks." Nearly two-thirds of those surveyed pointed to women having to try harder to "prove themselves." Today, people continue to view male and female leaders in different perspectives and within the framework of stereotypes, but the research reveals that women have particular positive traits and skills that can help them succeed personally and better society as a whole.[37]

---

36 Jack Zenge. . .oseph Folkman, "Research: Women Score Higher Than Men in Most Leadership Skills," *hbr.org*, June 25, 2019.

37 Pavithra Mohan, Study: Women rank better than men at these leadership traits, *fastcompany.com*, September 24, 2018.

Even the concept of execution in the sports realm can be compared for men and women. A working research publication from Ben-Gurion University of the Negev points to an interesting insight in the sports realm and the topic of "choking," or failing to perform under pressure. In analyzing close to 8,000 tennis matches, the researchers found that, "Comparing the performance of men versus women in low-stake versus high-stake situations, we find that men consistently choke under competitive pressure, but with regard to women, the results are mixed. Furthermore, even if women show a drop in performance in the more crucial stages of the contest, the drop is still about 50 percent smaller than that of men. These findings are robust to different specifications and estimation strategies."

The researchers point to the slower rate of cortisol increase in women compared to men as one possible reason that they are comparatively less likely to choke under pressure than men. Of course, the real world is undeniably more complicated than a tennis match, but what this points to is an interesting advantage that women might have: the ability to work well in high pressure situations.[38]

Clearly, the research on distinguishing different outcomes and attributes of men vs. women is plentiful. One more skill that women appear to be endowed with is a healthy level of confidence. A research article titled, "Boys Will Be Boys: Gender, Overconfidence, and Common Stock Investment" from 2001 explored differences on annual returns for male

---

38   Danny Cohen-Zada, Alex Krumer, Mosi Rosenboi...ffer Moshe Shapir, "Choking under Pressure and Gender," *Ben-Gurion University of the Negev*, September 27, 2016.

and female investors. It revealed that men tend to be more overconfident, trading 45 percent more often than women, yet earn lower returns after fees than women, at a statistically significant level of 1 percent.[39] Confidence might be key, but overconfidence does not seem to be so.

I could share many other examples, but I'll end here with one final example exploring the topic of cooperation for men and women. In 1993, some economists and psychologists studied this idea using a prisoner's dilemma experiment. Subjects played a game where if they and another subject choose to cooperate, they would receive a monetary reward. But if they chose to defect, while the other chose to cooperate, their payoff, in the form of the monetary reward, would be even higher. There exists a benefit in deploying a non-cooperative strategy here. From this experiment, it was found that men are 24 percent more likely to deploy the non-cooperative strategy than women, holding all other variables constant. What this implies, and what other research also supports, is that women tend to be more cooperative than men.[40]

I hope that from the historical mention to societies that were more equal in nature and the above research-driven accounts, you are able to get a better picture of the incredible abilities and advantages that women have, and how they can use them to their advantage in work, relationships, and life in general.

---

39 Brad M. Barbe. . .errance Odean, "BOYS WILL BE BOYS: GENDER, OVERCONFIDENCE, AND COMMON STOCK INVESTMENT," *The Quarterly Journal of Economics*, February 2001.

40 Robert H. Frank, Thomas Gilovich. . .ennis T. Regan, "Does Studying Economics Inhibit Cooperation?" *The Journal of Economic Perspectives*, Volume 7, Issue 2, (Spring, 1993), 159-171.

For all of the struggles that women have gone through throughout history up until this very day, as the expression coined by the modern feminist movement goes, "Nevertheless, she persisted." It's precisely these advantages that we'll be digging deeper into throughout the following chapters, and my hope is that you'll grasp how these advantages and capabilities can be applied to the topic of change and transformation for the women whose experiences we explore.

***

Coming back to Hans Christian Andersen's *The Little Mermaid*, there's one more relevant piece to the story. When the witch prepared the special potion for the Little Mermaid to drink, she warned the Little Mermaid that the transformation from mermaid to human would be painful, saying, "It will hurt you . . . as if a sharp sword passed through you."[41]

Although I've come to the realization that pain isn't the fundamental cause or input variable that necessitates change, what is often true is that change itself *can be painful.*

It's the female perspective on change, whether painful or not, that we'll be exploring from here on out. Whether it be from our own stories, the media, or research, something that seems to be apparent is even though The Female Condition exists, simultaneously, each woman has specific, measurable advantages and can develop them if she chooses to do so. Let's call this capability: *The Female Advantage.*

---

41 Hans Christian Anderson, *The Little Mermaid*, Hans Christian Andersen Centre at the University of Southern Denmark, 2014.

This advantage, as expressed in this book through women's conscious efforts to drive their own ability to pivot and deal with life's uncontrollable changes, is on full display in the stories you'll read through the next nine chapters. You'll hear a variety of insights and compelling stories about what principles various women have leaned into when experiencing a pivot, whether it be a small, negative change (*Lego*); a small, positive change (*lollipop*); a large, negative change (*life-threatening*); or a large, positive change (*lottery*).

As we move forward, I hope you find all of these stories to align with the concept of *The Female Advantage* and to be in congruence with my hypothesis that the major catalyst of success resides in a woman's ability to change and adapt, and that underlying her ability to change and adapt is not necessarily a critical threshold of pain to be exceeded, but instead, the execution of certain principles.

CHAPTER 2

SHE'S RESILIENT

———

To fight for change tomorrow, we need to build resilience today.
-SHERYL SANDBERG

It's canceled.

When I signed up for my first triathlon, I was feeling ambitious. I didn't consider the shorter options and set my eyes on the Olympic distance: A 0.93-mile swim and a 24.8-mile bike ride, followed by a 6.2-mile run.

I spent months training, waking up early beginning in the spring and throughout the summer to get in the runs, bikes, and swims necessary to properly prepare my mind and body for the race. I distinctively recall a certain Saturday morning over the summer when I was grinding my way through a brick workout, which essentially combines more than one part of the triathlon into a single workout. That particular morning I'd be attempting a bike-to-run brick, where I'd complete twenty miles on the bike, followed by a four-mile run.

I had read somewhere that the transitions, which is the time spent between each of the different parts of the triathlon, are critical and need to be practiced as if it were the real race, requiring both focus and planning. So, my strategy was to do just that. On that Saturday I left some water and my preferred form of workout fuel, applesauce, on the stairs leading into my apartment to properly set the stage, enabling me to practice this brick as if I were competing in the actual race.

Twenty miles later, I stormed through the door of my apartment, dashing down the stairs to the basement to park my bike, and ran back up the stairs to begin my run. In my mind, every second mattered, and the clock was ticking. When I got back up the stairs and squeezed some applesauce into my mouth in a manic rush, I looked up to see one of my roommates.

"What are you doing?"

Between exasperated breaths and sips of water, I tried to explain my plan to her. She looked mortified.

The rest of my training remained similar: focused, strategic, and intense. I embodied the essence of the Alexander Graham Bell quote, "Preparation is the key to success,"[42] and absorbed that belief into my subconscious. Nothing was going to stop me from succeeding on race day. . . or so I thought.

---

42   "Before anything else, preparation is the key to success.," *quotes.net.*

A few days before the race, I became aware of the excruciatingly high temperatures that were being forecasted. However, I had specifically trained for this possibility and had adapted well to the summer heat. I wasn't going to let this small annoyance (Lego-type change) impact me *negatively*.

I shortly thereafter received the dreaded email that read:

"Upon consultation with the event's Medical Team, local law enforcement, and local meteorologists, for your safety and the safety of volunteers and law enforcement, the decision has been made to modify the Challenge distance to a Sprint (Fit) distance."

In that moment, I was particularly upset. I didn't think it was fair for the race officials to undermine *my* training and *my* goals. I felt wholly disrespected. As my emotions began to subside, I saw the logic in the decision process, and yet, I still felt a desire to set out and do what I had intended. *Was I going to be a victim of these uncontrollable circumstances?* I thought through what I could control and what I could not control.

I realized I actually had a lot of choices, but ultimately arrived at three final options: I could choose to compete in the race and feel disappointed that my goal of completing a full Olympic triathlon was squelched. I could compete in the race and choose not to feel disappointed and be satisfied with completing half the distance I had trained for. Or, I could get a little more creative.

I chose to get a bit creative. Race day came, all had gone well, and I had aced my transitions and done well in the overall race itself. But after crossing the finish line, I wasn't quite finished. I arrived back to my apartment, grabbed my bike and helmet once again, which were still emblazoned with the race stickers and number labels, and then headed out on the all-familiar local multi-use path. I had plans to complete the full distance myself.

Sometime during the next 12.4 miles on the bike, I encountered some familiar faces: volunteers from the event on the trail, biking home themselves. They didn't explicitly say it, but their faces expressed it, in the same way my roommate had when I had stormed through the apartment door on that one Saturday just weeks before:

"What are you doing?"

This time I didn't have to explain myself. I was on a mission to finish what I had set out to do. As the temperatures rose well into the 90s, I completed the bike portion, and then parking my bike back in the basement one final time, I went back out on the trail to finish the 3.1 miles of running. I had successfully completed *my version* of an Olympic triathlon, but had more importantly learned an important life lesson about resilience and my power to use the "controllable" and "uncontrollable" changes in life to my own advantage.

Before this occurrence, I had already understood the art of dividing life's moments between those two dichotomies in order to help myself live the best way possible. But from this experience, I realized that there is overlap between what is controllable in life and what is not. Like the yin and yang symbol, I learned that within the uncontrollable parts of life exists very tangible things I can control, and vice versa. The power lies in being able to discern what opportunities lie in the uncontrollable. Using this concept has helped facilitate a psychological change in thought that still impacts me today. At the crux of this personal realization in regard to the concept of change laid the principle of resilience.

***

What inhibits our ability to practice resilience?

In a working paper by INSEAD, an international graduate business school, the topic of victim syndrome was investigated. The abstract describes victims as people who are constantly complaining because they feel as if they have no control over their circumstances. These people constantly point to external situations to explain their internal problems. They blame their family, friends, co-workers, or maybe even the deer that forced them to slam on their brakes as the root of their difficulties. Maybe you know a few people who meet these criteria. Or perhaps you can think of certain times in your own life when you yourself had fit this mold.

If you've tried to help a person with a victim mentality, you might find it hopeless. These people fail to listen to your advice or fully accept your help because they believe their problems are, as the report puts it, "unique and therefore insoluble," and may often treat an empathetic helper with hostility and spite. The world for someone with this mindset is a dark place because they believe every person and every situation is out to hurt and damage them. Their worldview becomes summed up in the phrase, "I am miserable, therefore I am." It's precisely this mental state that can prohibit us from practicing resilience in an ever-evolving world.

This illustration provides further context to what it means to have a victim mentality:

"John, the CEO of a sustainable energy company, was wondering about the best way to deal with Amelia, one of his vice presidents. Although she had many positive qualities, Amelia was very high maintenance. She took up more of his time than any of his other direct reports and managing her was far from being a pleasure—she was such a drama queen, making scenes if things didn't go her way. And it didn't take much to make her feel wronged.

John was puzzled why such a highly competent professional always needed to play the role of victim. How was it possible for someone so bright and so talented to be so blind to her own inappropriate behavior? It grated on John, who had been a great advocate of gender diversity in the firm, that whenever Amelia got herself into trouble, she always blamed the 'old boy' network. John knew that was a poor argument. None of the other women in the company had ever mentioned it. He had bent over backward to increase the ratio of women at senior management in the company. The idea that there was such a thing as an old boys' network in the company that was holding back women was ridiculous.

Meetings with Amelia were like walking on eggshells. Going through her biannual feedback report with her was the worst. You never knew how she was going to react. John genuinely dreaded these sessions. Telling her how she could have handled a specific situation more effectively was an exercise in master diplomacy.

And now it was time for Amelia's next appraisal. John was having sleepless nights. He still had vivid memories of Amelia's overblown reactions the last time he had given her what he thought was constructive feedback. When he talked about how a specific situation could have been handled more effectively, she went into overdrive, starting a heated argument about his input, and denying any responsibility for the way things had gotten out of hand. Couldn't she see how remarkable it was that every time something went wrong, it was always somebody else's fault? When John persisted and tried to show her that she had not just been an innocent bystander in the example he had given, Amelia lashed out at him, again presenting herself as a victim. After these exchanges, John would feel thoroughly miserable, wondering why he had bothered to go through the exercise in the first place. He felt as if he had victimized her. A typical feature of their particular pas de deux was that he would end up feeling sorry for her and try to calm her down. John wondered how effective this approach really was, as the same scenario kept on repeating itself."

This story, although a suitable illustration, is rather incomplete. What happened to Amelia that causes her to act the way she does? Was it something from her childhood? Or something she's struggling through personally right now? Clearly, a woman doesn't behave this way for her own enjoyment, right? I won't argue against the truth that this world is full of people who are genuine victims of unjust situations and unfathomably horrible circumstances. But what I will argue for is that the world at large would be a better place if more people sought to practice resilience as a way to transcend the victim mentality and push themselves to pivot.

What's even more insightful than the reality of these scenarios in which the victim mentality could prevail is *how* people are choosing to respond. Women in particular, as we'll see shortly with Martha's story, have a remarkable power to reframe difficult situations in a positive lens to avoid the victim mentality. Failing to take responsibility and accountability for our circumstances is what regresses us into the victim state. For me with my adjusted triathlon and Amelia in the example above, we were both functioning with non-ideal scenarios, but in my own example, I made a conscious choice to practice resilience, which led me to design my own triathlon, while Amelia did not seek such a change.

But perhaps, for example, Amelia had an abusive upbringing and the emotional trauma is beginning to resurface, or maybe she just went through a heart-wrenching breakup. As much as these potential scenarios could point to the reasoning behind her behavior and are no doubt valid conditions, they shouldn't be used as a perpetual excuse to her conduct, which had the adverse effects of causing anxiety and frustration for those she interacted with. The theme of making excuses and putting blame on the "uncontrollables" of one's life as a reason for ineffective behavior is a primary symptom of the victim mentality in action.

So how can we identify the victim mentality when it's occurring in ourselves or in others? INSEAD's working paper provides a checklist to see where a person might fit on the "victim syndrome scale." Some of the questions to ask are: Does every conversation end up centered on their problems? Do they always expect the worst? Do they believe that everyone else has an easier life? Do they never feel responsible for their negative behavior? Do they feel the world is out to get them?[43] From what we've seen, it is evident that a victim mentality can hold us back from experiencing change for ourselves and handling those external changes that are less controllable.

So then, how can we transcend a victim mentality and instead practice resilience?

Martha Sharkey serves as an inspiring example of a woman who chose to not give in to a victim mentality. Her story teaches us how we can use resilience as a springboard into new opportunities.

Is today a good day? Depending on who you ask, you'll get a variety of responses. However, for Martha, on any one day, she would say yes. She and her husband Paul are co-founders of Today Is A Good Day, a nonprofit that supports parents and families with premature newborns. Of course, there are days for Martha that do not quite fit the definition of a good day. Many could argue that Martha was perhaps a victim of horrible circumstances that she absolutely did not deserve. However, it was her resilience that helped her find new meaning and purpose in life in the midst of her struggles.

---

43 Manfred F. R. Kets de Vries, "Are Yo. . .ictim of Victim Syndrome?," *INSEAD*, 2012.

In 2010, she learned that she was expecting twins. Everything in the pregnancy was going along smoothly until Tuesday, November 9. Martha was working at the Franklin Institute in Philadelphia as the senior sales manager, and something just didn't feel quite right. Typical of any first-time mom, she called her doctor, who recommended she come in to make sure everything was okay. That day, Martha's life changed forever—as far as the framework goes—in a largely negative (*life-threatening*) way.

Five-and-a-half days after her arrival at the hospital, at just twenty-three weeks pregnant, she went into labor, delivering Claire and Mary. She recalls the day as a blur, saying, "Those were moments you'll never forget." She was rushed through the hallway by doctors and nurses, hoping to make it to the OR before Claire was delivered. Martha was put under anesthesia. When she awoke she was left wondering whether or not her daughters were alive.

Miraculously, they both were and had been immediately admitted to the neonatal intensive care unit. Claire was diagnosed with bilateral grades three and four brain bleeds, which are the two worst brain bleeds possible. Doctors advised Martha and Paul through the harsh reality that Claire could very well never walk, talk, or function as a normal human being later in life. Claire was not doing as well as Mary, but over the next two weeks, Mary developed an infection and her condition began to quickly worsen.

Just eighteen days after arriving into the world, on November 28, Mary "earned her angel wings." After that, Martha and her husband Paul were left with the all-consuming task of navigating the mourning process of losing a child while also focusing on Claire's growth and development.

It was during this time that Martha received a bracelet from a friend engraved with the phrase, "One Day at a Time." The Sharkeys used this phrase as their mantra over the next few months, as they watched and cheered as Claire slowly learned how to breath without a respirator, gain weight, feed from a bottle, and successfully move out of an isolette incubator. Eventually, the good days outweighed the bad. On February 25, 2011, after 103 days in the hospital, Claire's medical team announced, "Today was a good day", and Claire graduated from the NICU. Over three months after arriving into the world at Abington Memorial Hospital, a thriving Claire was released and sent home with Martha and Paul.

Martha refused to be a victim of her circumstances yet found her healing process while transitioning back into the "real world" to be a difficult one. During casual conversations at work or social events, people would ask her how many kids she had. Martha recalls, "When we first started our life with Claire at home, I would freely and openly go into our story with the person who was just trying to make small talk. I would share that we had identical twins and our stronger twin passed. I would overwhelm them with our journey as a way to help myself grieve and keep Mary's short but important life relevant. Often, people were left speechless, and had nothing to say except, 'I'm sorry.'"

As Claire grew and Martha continued through the grieving process, she was able to shift from a place of pain and sadness to one of growth and impact. From her resilience sprouted increased empathy for others going through their own life-changing experiences like hers.

For helping others through their own struggles of life and empowering them to practice resilience over a victim mentality, Martha says, "It's okay for you to say, 'I don't personally know what you're going through right now. But I want to let you know that I appreciate you sharing your story with me' . . . saying, 'Thank you for sharing your experience and your journey with me,' means the world."

Martha's advice is similar to Brene Brown's, a renowned psychologist who has focused her research on the topic of empathy. The skill of empathy can be employed to both avoid the victim mentality ourselves and to help others through their own challenges. Brown describes the four components of empathy as being able to put yourself in someone else's shoes, avoiding judgement, recognizing the emotion in another person, and communicating that you recognize that emotion.

These steps defy the less effective concept of sympathy, which Brown illustrates with the following scenario: Let's say a friend is stuck in a dark cave experiencing many emotions such as sadness, despair, or anxiety. Sympathy says, "I can help you, here, let me throw you a sandwich," while empathy says, "I can help you. I'm coming down the ladder."[44]

Empathy is not an uncontrollable. As with Martha's story, your capacity to empathize can grow. In a fascinating study, Dr. Jamil Zaki, a professor of psychology at Stanford

---

44   "Dr. Brené Brown: Empathy vs Sympathy," *twentyonetoys.com*.

University, explored the effect of labeling empathy to a group as a trait which cannot change versus a characteristic that can evolve. Those in the study were assigned to two groups to read articles with titles such as "Empathy, like Plaster, Is Pretty Stable over Time" and "Empathy is Changeable and Can Be Developed." After each group ran through an empathy "obstacle course," the data revealed that those who were primed to believe empathy was a changeable skill showed significantly more effort to understand others, such as their race or political views.[45]

The growth of empathy would be the cornerstone of Martha's pivot toward a new direction in her career. After all of their time in the hospital, Martha and Paul personally experienced the widespread emotional and financial needs of families navigating the NICU journey. This oftentimes left families without the resources, knowledge, and connections they required to take care of themselves and parent to their full potential. The realization of this disconnect served as the foundation of the launch of their nonprofit, Today Is A Good Day, in 2014.

Even after the launch of the nonprofit, Martha's story doesn't end quite yet. In 2015, Martha became pregnant again. After an anxious and stressful pregnancy, she gave birth full-term to Martha Rose. Three years later, in May of 2018, the Sharkeys found out the exciting news that they would be expecting once more.

---

45 TEDx Talks, "BUILDING EMPATHY: How to hack empathy and get others to care mor. . .amil Zak. . .EDxMarin," October 18, 2017, video, 13:18.

However, a few months into this pregnancy, they were informed with the devastating news that their baby boy, named William, had a very rare chromosomal abnormality called Trisomy 18. This abnormality meant that William would most likely die in utero or within the first year of life. Visibly pregnant and receiving congratulations, Martha had to navigate the incredibly difficult process of sharing William's terminal diagnosis with friends and family.

On Monday, December 17 at 9:38 a.m., William was born weighing 2 lb. and 4 oz. He lived for ninety-one minutes. His sisters showered him with hugs and kisses. They read him books and sang songs to him. Martha describes the pain she felt: "It's hard to put into words the feeling of holding our second child as he passed away in our arms. This is a challenging road to travel. Two of our four children have died… half of our children is a very difficult realization to process."

The Sharkeys' experience is far from typical, yet the essence of Martha's story is relevant for all. Claire and Martha Rose, now nine and four, are frequent visitors to the cemetery and have a knowledge of death far beyond the norm of other kids their age. Oftentimes, Claire and Martha Rose sit near Mary or William's gravesite, eating donut holes or playing with their toys on a quiet Sunday morning.

When Martha and Paul were in the NICU supporting Claire for three months, they took each day at a time, celebrating the small wins, like making it to the milestone of lunchtime. Martha's growth and healing evolved throughout her life's experiences, and in her words, "Sometimes you just power through the grieving and the trauma of it all and it doesn't necessarily hit you until you're down the road and away from it and you can look back on it."

Despite all of the challenges Martha has faced, she serves as a shining example of someone who embodies *The Female Advantage* by refusing to succumb to a victim mentality by practicing resiliency to overcome even those "life-threatening" circumstances. Within her resiliency, she realized the advantage of sharing empathy with others in similar circumstances, which spurred the creation of her nonprofit. Sheryl Sandberg calls this "post-traumatic growth." This growth comes from someone who is able to navigate through the pain and traumas of their life in effective ways. Its precursor is "pre-traumatic growth," which encompasses the concept of building resilience on a day-to-day basis.[46] For each of us, the power lies in our ability to respond to our circumstances with resilience, and then choosing to allow our circumstances to lead us to pivoting toward potentially new opportunities.

***

When attempting to transcend a victim mentality in my own life and choose resilience, I'm reminded of a quote by Ghanaian writer Ernest Agyemang Yeboah. He says:

"Thought is uncontrollable but controllable. Thought is the pivot of life and the epitome of good or bad living. A controlled thought is a controlled life and an uncontrolled life is an uncontrolled living. Our first and last thoughts from dawn

---

46   Jan Bruce, "Sheryl Sandberg's Guide to Grief, Growth and Getting It Right in Today's Business Climate," *Forbes.com*, August 25, 2017.

to dusk are of great essence to living a purposeful life. They form a catalyst for a progressive or retrogressive life. What do you think of most before you sleep? What do you ponder upon most upon waking up from bed? The distinctive boundaries to your purposeful day are your first and last thoughts of the day. Remember! The first and the last thoughts."[47]

Our thoughts control us, yet we have the ability to control our thoughts. We can't control every circumstance in our lives, but we can control how we choose to respond to them. If a change in thought occurs, and if we're under the assumption that thoughts pave the way to actions, then to change our thoughts should mean to redirect our actions, or in other words, to pivot. This means that the choice to move away from, or avoid, a victim mentality begins right between our ears, in our minds' power to choose resilience.

---

47 "Purposeful Quotes," *jarofquotes.com.*

CHAPTER 3

SHE'S GRITTY

The most difficult thing is the decision to act. The rest is merely tenacity.

-AMELIA EARHART

In 1973, two housewives in the small town of Brookfield, Wisconsin, were tasked with helping their sons with a Cub Scout project. During this project, housewives Betty Morris and Kate Bloomberg recalled a magazine that provided instructions on how to make tiny charms by drawing on plastic lids and baking them in an oven. Other than realizing this process to simply be the perfect art project for their two sons, Betty and Kate saw that this craft could be transformed into a potentially profitable business opportunity.[48]

But there was one large problem. The initial upstart required the purchase of a hefty 1,000-pound roll of polystyrene plastic that provided the perfect amount of shrinkage when

---

48 Saffron Sener, "Shrinky Dinks. . .ove Story," *baremagazine.org*, October 3, 2018.

heated. They took the risk and purchased the entire roll. They then soon began testing the market by selling their product, coined "Creative Shrinky Dinks Packs," at local shopping malls for two dollars apiece. They had a surprising amount of success. In fact, these entrepreneurs had so much business in the first few months that the local Sears ran out of the permanent ink markers required to draw the designs onto the Shrinky Dinks.

In just five months, more than $150,000 of the plastic shrinking toy was sold across twenty-six stores. Eventually, Shrinky Dinks were licensed by major toy companies at the time like Milton Bradley, Colorforms, and Skyline Toys.[49] Without the risk-taking ability and resourcefulness of two women in small-town America during the bell bottoms and disco era, millions of children all around the world wouldn't have had the joy of playing with this beloved product. But perhaps even more so, Michelle Khine, who was just a kid at the time of the Shrinky Dinks craze, wouldn't have been able to conduct her ground-breaking nanotechnology research in the 2000s.

Over thirty years after the invention of Shrinky Dinks, Michelle was asked, "What's the secret to your success?" And her response is as follows:

"I'm very persistent. I don't give up. I think that's the key to being an entrepreneur. Growing up, nobody thought I was smart. My teachers thought I had learning difficulties. I left

---

49 "Vintage Shrinky Dinks: How these crafty toys were invente. . .ow they work," *clickamericana.com.*

my ego at the door very early on in my life so when people said I was stupid, or my idea was crazy, or it wouldn't work, it never bothered me. I used that as constructive fodder to try to improve on the idea or to try to figure out how to do it better and not give up on my long-term goal."[50]

For Michelle, it would be her grit that would lead her to success and creative problem-solving, with Shrinky Dinks as her inspiration.

***

In 2005, Michelle entered her makeshift lab at the University of California, Merced, to conduct her research. However, the research she was conducting required specialized equipment, and her current improvised setup did not provide the functionality she needed.

Michelle self-proclaims as being "not a patient person," so when faced with the limitations of a lab that didn't fit her research requirements, she was urged to think more creatively about solutions to her problem. Something needed to change because her current setup was not conducive to her being able to complete her research successfully.

Michelle refused to give up and, instead of thinking about what she *didn't* have in her lab, she thought about what she *did* have. There were just a few things at her disposal: a toaster oven, a laser printer, and some plastic. In her desperation,

---

50 Dr. Michelle Khine, Scientist and Innovator Dr. Michelle Khine: "Growing Up, Nobody Though. . .as Smart," *forbes.com*, March 22, 2018.

she remembered her favorite childhood toy: Shrinky Dinks. Could she use the same concept for her research?

Turns out, she could. By starting big and then shrinking her nano-chips down via polystyrene plastic, she found the perfect loophole to not let her limited resources restrain her research. For Michelle, *The Female Advantage* of practicing grit brought her to an intriguingly unconventional place: the intersection of Shrinky Dinks and nanotechnology.[51]

Michelle's own ability to persist and refusal to give up are the central reasons for her research's success. More so, her persistence catalyzed the success of other engineers and researchers all across the globe. The seemingly small and annoying environmental change of having to conduct her research in a makeshift lab was—according to the framework—a "Lego" type change. Yet, the application of grit within the nuisance of an ill-equipped lab would have largely positive implications.

The discovery of the application of Shrinky Dinks in nanotechnology quickly became viral in the research realm, resulting in numerous labs changing current practices and instead adopting Michelle's techniques for their own research. One of the which was Harvard's Microrobotics Laboratory, which used Shrinky Dinks to build self-assembling robots.[52]

***

---

51 Aaron Rowe, "Hack: Young Professor Makes Lab-on-a-Chip with Shrinky Dink and Toaster Oven," *wired.com,* December 4, 2007.

52 Sebastian Anthony, "Harvar...IT create first self-assembling robots—the first real Transformers," *extremetech.com,* August 8, 2014.

We don't have to look very many degrees beyond Michelle to find other females practicing grit as a principle to realizing change. A few years after her discovery, in Nashville, Tennessee, a young girl named Gitanjali Rao asked, "Why not use carbon nanotube sensors to detect lead in water?" Her inquiry didn't arise spontaneously. While the engineers in Harvard's Microrobotics Lab were busy designing their self-assembling robots inspired by Michelle's research breakthrough, just a short walk away, engineers in MIT's Deshpande Center for Technological Innovation were trying to solve a different problem: creating an inexpensive hazardous chemical detector that could be worn by soldiers.

The resulting invention was low-cost electrophilic carbon nanotubes that detect trace amounts of toxins in the environment and transmit the data to a local device. These sensors are highly sensitive, able to detect less than ten parts per million of toxic gases in less than five seconds. Additionally, the sensors are highly economical, costing about five cents to make, far less expensive than laboratory technology that yields the same results.[53]

Similar to how other nanotechnology labs adopted Michelle's Shrinky Dink methodologies, Gitanjali herself sought to apply MIT's carbon nanotube concept in a different context. This invention would inspire young Gitanjali to spearhead breakthroughs in water consumption safety.

---

53 Rob Matheson, "Wireless, wearable toxic-gas detector," *news.mit.edu*, June 20, 2016.

Growing up, Gitanjali's closest friends would often ask her why she was out of town. It wasn't for any kind of vacation. It was for keynote addresses on the topics of environmentalism and water safety—two things she is particularly passionate about. All of these speaking opportunities involving prominent scientists and research organizations weren't always the norm, however. Gitanjali, now fourteen years old, had to work tirelessly, getting gritty and adopting new strategies, to get to where she is today and to make the impact she has.

She has learned a lot in her relatively short existence so far, but no one had to teach her how to fall in love with the sciences and experimentation. It all began when she was just three years old, when her uncle gifted Gitanjali her first chemistry kit and, as she put it, "I completely wrecked it." After completing all of the experiments, and a few of her own imagination, she craved more.

Specifically, what caught her attention was the physical changes that she could produce with certain chemicals and the ability to witness the results with her own eyes. Those fundamentally basic, vinegar-and-baking-soda-type experiments were what hooked Gitanjali on the concept of science. Since the days of making a mess with her first ever chemistry kit, every year after that, she would ask for another one to dig her hands into.

Since wrecking those first few kits, Gitanjali has been completing about one new invention every year. Most recently, her passions and skillset specifically aligned to combatting Flint, Michigan's water crisis, and this particular project is where MIT's research with nanotubes inspired her to make an impact in the Flint community.

The inspiration started after watching her parents run a water test in their home in Denver, Colorado. She witnessed the inefficiency of the process herself, which can be both slow and inaccurate. She thought, "Well, this is not a reliable process." It was after further research that she was left feeling "appalled by the number of people affected by lead contamination in water" and "wanted to do something to change this."

She began researching where lead contamination was the most prolific and landed on Flint, Michigan. The Flint water crisis began in 2014 when the city switched its water supply to the Flint River in a cost-saving effort. However, this water was not properly tested or treated, which resulted in contaminated water being pumped into residents' homes.

The simple task of taking a shower was lost by some. Resident Rhonda Kelso says, "The water, it burns our eyes. It's horrifying." The lives of those affected have significantly changed, and resident Anthony Lyons describes the logistics of locating and using water as "a second job." Even children's leisure time has been impacted, as Lomalinda Morrison says: "It makes it hard, because kids like to play in water."[54]

What led Gitanjali to tackle the Flint's crisis in particular is the fact that Flint is one of the worst places in the United States for lead contamination. Flint's water has been

---

54   Jake May, "Still standing: Flint residents tell their stories about living with poisoned water," *mlive.com.*

measured to contain 127 parts per billion of lead, which is well above the US Environmental Protection Agency's standards of fifteen parts per billion. Additionally, children are acutely vulnerable to lead, due do absorbing four-to-five times as much as adults, which can cause brain and nervous system problems ranging from headaches and nausea to seizures and even death.[55] As a Flint pediatrician puts it, "Lead is one of the most damning things you can do to a child in their entire life-course trajectory."

Unfortunately, the crisis in Flint is only getting worse, as reports in 2015 found elevated levels of lead in residents' blood samples citywide, which doubled from the amount of reports in 2014.[56] Clearly, this is a major problem that needs to be solved. Unfortunately, a poor government response meant that residents were stuck with a major problem that they alone weren't able to ameliorate. With a population close to one hundred thousand, Gitanjali faces a substantial issue and would have to get her "hands dirty"—just like she did with all of those science kits growing up—in order to help solve it.

To get started with the daunting task of attempting to find a solution to this major problem, she learned more and more about water and studied the past civilizations that had state-of-the-art irrigation systems. She learned of the ancient Greeks, who created a goddess and subsequent story for this basic human need. Derived from the Greek word "*têthê*," which means "nurse" or "grandmother," Tethys was a titan

55 "Lead poisoning and health," *who.int*, August 23, 2019.
56 Melissa Denchak, "Flint Water Crisis: Everything You Need to Know," *nrdc.org*, November 8, 2018.

goddess of fresh water.[57] In an island landscape, surrounded by the undrinkable salt-water of the Ionian, Mediterranean, and Aegean Sea on all sides, Crete, a major metropolis city of ancient Greece, would have been at a disadvantage in regard to its initial endowment of fresh drinking water. Nonetheless, they managed to design advanced water and irrigation systems only bested thousands of years later in the late 19th century in Europe and America.[58] However, in 21st century Michigan, Gitanjali leaned that this wasn't the case.

Borrowing the namesake of the ancient goddess and inspired by the ancient Greeks themselves, Gitanjali developed Tethys, a portable lead detection device. Again, she asked the seemingly simple question after being inspired by the MIT scientists' research: *"Why not use carbon nanotube sensors to detect lead in water?"*

That question brought her into the thick of things in her lab, where she would begin iterating on her invention and testing her device. On the chemical level, similar to the MIT scientists, she found success in her invention by stacking carbon atoms in a beehive shape, creating a nanotube. The nanotube then responds to changes in electron flow which occurs if lead exists in water. Tethys can measure the amount of lead in the water and relay the information to a smartphone app. Hypothetically, the residents of Flint could use Tethys in their homes to track the levels of lead in water, and Flint's government could collect the data on lead levels to help determine "hot spots" of high levels of lead in water throughout the city.

57 "TETHYS," *theoi.com.*
58 E.G. Dialynu. . ..N. Angelakis, "The Evolution of Water Supply Technologies in Ancient Crete, Greece," *worldwatermuseum.com.*

After hours in the lab conducting meticulous research, her device worked, but it needed to be run through various tests to guarantee its accuracy. At the time, Gitanjali was using her home as her makeshift lab, but she needed a proper laboratory in which to validate her device. Similarly to Michelle in her unsuitable lab, Gitanjali's current set up wasn't going to work, and she knew she had to think creatively to solve her problem.

So, she got gritty, sending not ten or twenty, but hundreds of emails to various labs across the country. She boldly asked for a chance to test her device, but struggled to prove that she, in her own words, "Wasn't just a kid trying to do a science project." Instead, she was a young scientist, "trying to make an impact."

Unfortunately, she wasn't receiving many replies, and the responses she was generating for the most part stated things like, "Unfortunately, we don't have the time or resources to undertake this project."

Nonetheless, Gitanjali persisted, continuing to send email after email in an effort to find a proper lab. Finally, in 2017, after winning the Young Scientist Challenge, a highly competitive innovation challenge for fifth-to-eighth graders, she garnered more respect and interest from the science community.[59] Denver Water, which serves high quality water to 1.4 million people, took an interest in her work and invited her to tour their lab.

_____

59   "Challenge Participants," *youngscientistlab.com*.

After the tour, Gitanjali emailed Denver Water and asked, like she had hundreds of times before, if they would consider opening up their Water Quality Lab for her testing procedures. This time though, she was successful, and Denver Water said yes. Since then, she has been working with Denver Water and their research team to test and perfect her device, in preparation for field testing in Flint.

For Gitanjali, her work on Tethys and her various other inventions are inspired by many female scientists that have come before her, specifically Nobel Prize-winning Marie Curie, not only for her scientific discoveries, but for how, as Gitanjali puts it, "She put others' lives before her own."

Marie and her husband Pierre were awarded the Nobel Prize for Physics in 1903 for the discovery of polonium and radium. In 1906, Pierre tragically died in a freak accident and Marie assumed his responsibilities as teacher at the Sorbonne in France, becoming the first woman to teach there. Marie continued her research and was awarded her own Nobel Prize in Chemistry in 1911. Along with her awards, her research was crucial for real world applications and innovations in World War I such as the development of x-rays in surgery, which were equipped to ambulances that Marie herself drove onto the front lines of war.[60]

Similar to Gitanjali's uneven path for inventing Tethys, both of these women's efforts, and the concept of grit at large in respect to generating change, can be described in Marie's words:

---

60 "Marie Curie (186. . .934)," *bbc.co.uk.*

"We must not forget that when radium was discovered no one knew that it would prove useful in hospitals. The work was one of pure science. And this is a proof that scientific work must not be considered from the point of view of the direct usefulness of it. It must be done for itself, for the beauty of science, and then there is always the chance that a scientific discovery may become like the radium a benefit for mankind."[61]

For Gitanjali, Tethys isn't her life's only work. Plenty of other topics and issues interest her as well. She's fascinated with the topic of gene editing and is excited that another gene related to cystic fibrosis was recently mapped, which could lead to better design and development of treatments, and potentially even be utilized to determine a cure for the disease in the near future. Some other passion projects of hers that will be developed within the next few years are a device that can help diagnose prescription opioid addiction, as well as a smartphone application that can protect and prevent cyber bullying.

Gitanjali's practice of grit and persistence brought her through her original beta versions of Tethys all the way to a completed product. She's learned how to use the changes in her life, whether negative like the continual rejection from labs all across the country, or greatly positive, and lottery-esque in nature, like finally receiving the news that Denver Water would allow her to use their facilities, as opportunities to continually practice grit.

---

61   Asad Meah, "35 Inspirational Marie Curie Quotes on Success," *awakenthegreatnesswithin.com.*

Whether it be through Gitanjali's personal experiences or her professional scientific endeavors in experimentation and invention, she will continue to use adaptability and perseverance as enablers to her success in the future. Along the way, her path wasn't simple and smooth. She created a working prototype, attempted to find a lab, and never gave up. She wasn't afraid to use her voice and make conscious pivots along the way, embracing change as a way to help her achieve her goals.

**

How can I practice grit?

Persistence, tenacity, and grit are different words with similar results. They all result in certain outcomes and successes that are generated by input that requires a high level of commitment and significant investments in time and energy. Marie Curie herself puts it this way, "Life is not easy for any of us. But what of that? We must have perseverance, and above all, confidence in ourselves."[62]

Angela Duckworth could very easily be called the "Queen of Grit," as she's dedicated most of her life's work to this single concept. When she talks about grit, she doesn't just mean hard work and commitment. She also attributes the concept of passion to the idea of grit.

Her own interest in the topic arose when she noticed a fascinating dichotomy while teaching middle and high school

---

62   "Marie Curie Forbes Quotes," *forbes.com.*

students. The most talented students weren't necessarily the ones who performed the best academically. Her research accredits grit as the explanation for the lack of correlation between IQ and performance. She points to four characteristics in those who have a high level of grit:[63]

1. You have something you find enduringly fascinating: Take a mental voyage back to your adolescent self. What did you find of extreme interest? What do you find yourself losing track of time in? For Gitanjali, it all began with those science kits as a child.

2. You view frustrations as a necessary part of the process: In the movie *Apollo 13*, Ed Harris, who was acting as Gene Kranz, chief flight director of the Apollo and Gemini programs, famously said, "Failure is not an option."[64] In the context of the movie, and space travel in general, that quote is most fitting. However, most daily activities we take part in are not life or death, or make or break for that matter. Duckworth believes the perception and reframing of failure in our lives is a key component to cultivating grit. When was the last time you embraced an opportunity in which you weren't entirely sure you would succeed? When the two founders of Shrinky Dinks purchased the 1,000-pound roll of plastic, I surmise they had absolutely no idea whether or not their business idea would be successful.

3. You look for ways to make work more meaningful: An experiment at Google asked employees to redefine their job responsibilities in a way that made them appear more

63   Robin Hilmantel, "4 Signs You Have Grit," *time.com*, May 12, 2016.
64   Movieclips, "Apollo 13 (1995)—Failure Is Not an Option Scene (6/11. . .ovieclips," August 3, 2017, video, 2:09.

meaningful. What Google found was that employees were able to increase job satisfaction and performance just by "rethinking" about their duties in a more purposeful lens.[65] For Gitanjali, she found the application of the nanotube technology to solve Flint's water crisis to be the most impactful option that suited her skills and passions.

4. You believe you can change and grow: Dr. Carol Dweck, a psychologist at Stanford, found that people with a growth mindset put in more time and effort at work and have more resilience.[66] How have you utilized a growth mindset when undergoing external changes or to catalyze your own change within yourself? Personally, I credit much of the success I've had in life to my belief in my own ability to change, adapt, and grow.

Duckworth's research points to the conclusion that grit is a characteristic that can be nurtured and developed consciously throughout one's life. She explains that to make a pivot toward practicing grit, one should first and foremost pursue what interests them, then practice those pursuits, seek to find purpose in their work, and have hope.

For pursuing those things that interest you, inquiry is an instrumental variable here. You don't need to go on a soul-searching mission to find your interests. Instead, think about what *might* be of interest to you and seek it out with child-like curiosity. Whether it's rock climbing, ballroom dancing, or blogging, tackle one or more areas of interest,

---

65 Robin Hilmantel, "4 Signs You Have Grit," *time.com*, May 12, 2016.

66 Carol Dweck, "What Havin. . .Growth Mindset" Actually Means," *hbr. org*, January 13, 2016.

not because it's something you can "check off the list," but instead, doing so simply because you can.

Regarding the idea of practice, Dr. Adam Grant, renowned organizational psychologist and professor, believes interest precedes talent. Under this assumption, you might not be the best at whatever you're trying to accomplish, but you shouldn't let that stop you. Let that inspire you on the never-ending journey of continuous improvement. The word "practice" itself implies that there is something to be improved upon, and that's okay. James Waters, former Navy SEAL, describes this concept like this: "One of the key strengths of the SEAL Teams is the culture of constant self-improvement. No one ever says, 'That's good enough.' On almost every real world mission I was on—even the most successful ones—we spent 90 percent of our post-mission debrief focusing on what we did wrong or could have done better."[67]

For finding purpose, there's a lot of research that suggests those who are focused on helping others achieve their goals are happier themselves (and we'll dig deeper into this in Chapter 7). Like characteristic #3 above, Duckworth herself says, "What ripens passion is the conviction that your work matters. For most people, interest without purpose is nearly impossible to sustain for a lifetime. It is therefore imperative that you identify your work as both personally interesting and, at the same time, integrally connected to the well-being of others."[68]

---

67 Eric Barker, "A Navy SEAL explains 8 secrets to grit and resilience," *theladders.com*, June 5, 2019.

68 Angela Duckworth, Grit: The Power of Passion and Perseverance, (New York, Scribner, 2016.)

For the concept of hope, it doesn't necessarily mean to reck-lessly depend on tomorrow, next week, or next year to be dramatically better than any part of your life today. Instead, hope is about cultivating the effort required today as the security deposit to that experience, that thing, or that feeling you hope to have at a future time. For Gitanjali, for example, this looked like sending out hundreds of emails to labs all over the country. Hope is critical, as research found that those with lower levels of hope set lower goals and were less motivated to continue if they failed.

The housewives who invented Shrinky Dinks in 1973 didn't quite have Duckworth's frameworks printed out and memo-rized by heart, but I would surmise that if you asked either of them today what top skills they thought helped bring Shrinky Dinks to international recognition, one of them would surely say grit.

All the way from the legendary plastic of the 70s, to Michelle's application of that plastic in nanotechnology, through four-teen-year-old Gitanjali's Tethys invention today, it's clear that grit is a catalyst to the embodiment of *The Female Advantage*, as within this practice women can effectively realize change and adapt to external changes that aren't quite as controllable. As we've discovered, these women were able to utilize their inquisitiveness to begin their inquiry, but grittiness is what led them to adapt and pivot along the way toward reaching their goals.

Where can you find grit in action? Probably in a lot of places, but as we've seen, it's particularly apparent in those women who persevered on their way toward an ambitious goal. The concept of grit today is best epitomized by Dr. Martin Luther King Jr. when he proclaimed, "If you can't fly, then run, if you can't run, then walk, if you can't walk, then crawl, but whatever you do, you have to keep moving forward."[69]

---

69 "Martin Luther King Jr.," *wisdomtoinspire.com.*

CHAPTER 4

SHE QUESTIONS

———

The important thing is not to stop questioning. Curiosity has its own reason for existing.

-ALBERT EINSTEIN

"How come she has more homework than me?"

That was the question. In the fifth grade, I attended a private school, while my neighbor, Julia, attended the local public middle school. Each day after I got off the school bus, I'd walk over to Julia's house and ask her to play outside with me. It didn't take very long for me to recognize a certain pattern:

"I wish we could play together, but I have homework to do."

I was confused as to why I had no more than twenty minutes of homework each day, while Julia seemingly had hours. I was breezing through my times tables, but something still wasn't quite adding up. As I began to inquire further about the academic obstacles keeping her from playing with me, I found out some novel information:

Highland Middle School has accelerated math.

I never knew such a program even existed. From this new-found data I started to map out my action plan to switch schools and went to my parents with the news.

I want more homework so I'm changing schools.

After many hard-fought conversations and a mastering of my negotiation skills, my mom and dad finally obliged. That fall, I would attend Highland Middle School.

This story is quite comedic to look back on (what fifth grader wants homework?), but it serves as the earliest memory in my life of my *questioning* leading me down a significantly *new path*. My life today could very well be vastly different if I had stayed at the private school. The fact that a simple question led me to such a largely positive, *lottery-type* change goes to show that the ability to ask questions is powerful in helping us achieve a pivot.

Oftentimes, it's precisely those questions, even though they may be simplistic in nature, that lead women to incredible discoveries, either about themselves or about the world. So logically then, there exists a real cost to not asking questions. Let me describe this cost of not questioning through a historical illustration.

Norse sailor Bjarni Herjólfsson experienced this cost himself around 980 AD. While taking part in his annual voyage from Scandinavia to Iceland, he received the news that his father had migrated to Greenland. So, he recalibrated his travel plans and set sail there instead.

During his voyage, he was met with treacherous storms that veered him off course for several days. As the story goes, once the bad weather subsided, he caught a view of something that didn't fit the description of what the other sailors had described as being Greenland. Perplexed, he described what he saw as being "wooded and having low hills." It wasn't Greenland, it was North America.[70]

His crew yearned to explore this untouched land, but he refused. Instead, he turned away from this land, staying unwaveringly committed to the mission of meeting his father. The *Sagas of the Greenlanders*, a compilation of Norse history written in the thirteenth or fourteenth century, describes Bjarni as being "short on curiosity," since he didn't take the once-in-a-lifetime opportunity to explore the unknown and pivot from his current trajectory into a new one.[71] We don't know what would have happened if Bjarni instead chose to explore this land, but I surmise it would've been a *lottery-type* change not only for Bjarni himself, but the Greenlanders at large.

What if, upon viewing that wooded and hilly land, Bjarni didn't turn away? What if he had asked:

---

70 T.J. Oleson, "BJARNI, HERJÓLFSSON," *Dictionary of Canadian Biography*, vol. 1, University of Toronto/Université Laval, 2003–, accessed September 3, 2019.

71 "SHORT ON CURIOSITY: THE STORY OF BJARNI JERJOLFSSON," Ultimate History Project, accessed September 3, 2019.

"What if we explored this land instead?"

Close to 2,500 years before Bjarni made the decision to stay on his course to Greenland, a different group of people on the other side of the globe were mastering the concept of wayfaring and exploring the unexplored.

The Polynesian Wayfinders' explorational success was built on the simple question:

"What if?"

While Europeans at the time were still clinging to shore, the Polynesians saw the water as an open highway. It was almost as if the ocean itself was inviting them on a journey of discovery. However, their traversals between Hawaii, New Zealand, and Easter Island in as early as 1500 BC were not simple or seamless.[72] It took collective efforts between ship building and knowledge transfer to make their trips successful, so they would eventually become known as "the greatest mariners the world has ever seen."[73]

How did they beat every other group of people to exploring the islands in the Pacific Ocean by thousands of years?

Undoubtedly, they had a geographic advantage, having originated from that region of the world to start. There are probably many other factors too, but one thing that seems apparent is that these people had a passion for inquiry. Unlike Bjarni,

---

72 "Polynesian History and Origin," PBS, accessed September 3, 2019.

73 "Polynesian Wayfinders," Solar Dynamics Observatory, video, April 10, 2012.

the Polynesians weren't afraid, or too committed to their current trajectory to ask, *"What if?"* and readjust their plans accordingly. Bjarni saw something unknown and turned away, but the Polynesians, similar to my fifth-grade self, embraced ambiguity and aimed their ships directly at the unknown.

***

As we've seen, in terms of changing directions both literally and metaphorically, there's power in asking questions and sometimes a large tradeoff if we do not. American psychologist Sue Savage-Rumbaugh sought to research the concept of question asking and communication through her research on Kanzi and his family. In the early 1980s during her research, when Kanzi was an infant, he observed his mother communicate using a special keyboard with geometric symbols. Kanzi's mother wasn't able to understand the communication device very well, but while Kanzi was seemingly playing in the background while the tests were being conducted, he began to pick up the idiosyncrasies of the device.

Over time, he was able to communicate using 348 symbols including food items, activities, and abstract concepts like "good" and "bad." To continue the groundbreaking research, Kanzi and some of his family and friends moved into a $10 million, eighteen-room house in Iowa. He and his family and friends spent their days simply, sprawled on the floor eating blueberries or M&Ms and enjoying movies like *The Legend of Tarzan.*

If you haven't figured it out yet, Kanzi is not a human, but he can still teach us a lot about inquiry and the power of asking questions. Kanzi is a bonobo, an endangered species of chimpanzee. What was uncovered through Sue's research was, in terms of asking questions, is that the main difference between our biological cousin Kanzi and ourselves is that humans understand that there is more information available to us in the world if we inquire.

Kanzi could ask for a banana or his friend, but he never asked, "Why is a banana yellow?" or "How does a banana get processed by my digestive system?" Kanzi simply doesn't have the mental capacity to even begin to conceive his own ignorance about the world around him.[74]

Similarly to Bjarni contrasted to the Polynesian Wayfinders, Kanzi provides us another interesting juxtaposition between the power of inquiry in bonobos to humans. Within the sect of humans themselves, toddlers provide us an excellent example of unapologetic question-asking ability.

Young children have the fearlessness to ask astoundingly outlandish questions. After analyzing hundreds of hours of recordings of children interacting with their parents for her PhD dissertation, psychologist Michelle Chouinard found an inflection point: Around the age of 2.5 years, toddler questions move from asking *what* and *where*, (*What is a monkey and where do they live?*), to *why* and *how* (*Why do monkeys have big ears and how come they aren't rainbow colored?*). [75]

---

74 Paul Raffaele, "Speaking Bonobo," *Smithsonian Magazine*, November 2006

75 Michelle M. Chouinard, *Children's Questions* (Wiley-Blackwell).

Up until about thirty months old, the toddlers' questions had been Kanzi-esque in nature, eliciting tangible, clear answers. After thirty months, these questions evolve to ones in which more extensive, abstract explanations are required. It's easy to take the ability to ask questions for granted, but we are the only species with an intellectual capacity advanced enough to ask *these kinds* of questions.

The questions that come out of toddlers aren't particularly profound or insightful, yet, it's the fearlessness in which they ask the question that can inspire each of us to speak up and question for ourselves.

This idea of asking questions and the power it has reminds me of a story by current COO of Facebook, Sheryl Sandberg, who, after giving a talk at work, was greeted by one of the audience members afterward. The female audience member told Sandberg, "I learned something today. I learned that I need to keep my hand up." The woman goes on to describe that during the Q&A portion, Sandberg said she'd take two more questions, and after the second one was asked, all of the women in the room put their hands down. However, several men kept their hands raised, and Sandberg continued to field their questions.[76]

The next time you internally debate whether or not to even ask a question, whether that be to a superior at work, or at a Q&A session with your favorite comedian, perhaps it would do you some good to contemplate the enormity of the

---

76 TED, "Why we have too few women leaders," Sheryl Sandberg, December 21, 2010, video.

fact that we are capable of even doing so in the first place. It's actually quite amazing. What can be even more powerful than asking questions though, is asking the *right kinds* of questions.

***

Roshi Givechi, former partner and executive design director at IDEO, a global design consulting firm credited for major innovations like the Apple computer mouse and insulin pens, is a woman who embodies *The Female Advantage* of inquiry in generating change. During her time at IDEO, working across various projects, partner Duane Bray said, "She's incredibly skilled at unlocking teams, asking questions that connect people and open possibilities."

Givechi doesn't fit the stereotypical designer or artist mold of projecting theatric energy or a whimsical spirit like your high school art teacher might have. She's curt, unassuming, and uncharismatic. She even self-proclaims as being "not the chattiest person." However, she's exceptionally talented at asking the right kinds of questions. As she puts it, "They're usually questions that might seem obvious or simple or unnecessary." But she says she "loves asking them because I'm trying to understand what's really going on."

The bulk of her question asking takes place in what IDEO calls Flights, or team meetings that occur throughout a project's lifespan. It's in these Flights that Givechi seeks to unearth tensions and help the group develop clarity and direction for the project. She listens intently, utilizing micro expressions like head nods and tilts, and is wholly comfortable with sitting in silence. Givechi uses a plethora of techniques that show the person she's working with that she genuinely cares about solving the problem, and for her, similar to the Polynesian Wayfinders on their journey to colonizing new islands, she says, "It's not about decisiveness. It's about discovery. For me, that has to do with asking the right questions the right way."[77] In these questions new insights are uncovered, leading to both small (*lollipop*) and large-type (*lottery*) positive changes in projects or inventions that would not have occurred otherwise.

As we've seen, there's a risk in not asking questions. But there's also a risk in asking questions. One Harvard Business School study found that the most prominent reason why people refrained from asking questions was due to fear of a negative evaluation.[78] Givechi serves as an inspiration of our ability to change the way we go about the process of question asking and helps us forfeit those fears we might have of possibly looking stupid when doing so.

Looking stupid? I could NEVER!

On the relational level, you might know of the invasion of privacy you've felt from a person you just met asking you question upon question. Or, maybe you have more memorable experiences with those people who fail to ask you a single question over the course of an entire conversation. In both dichotomies, there exists opportunity for *you* to become

---

77 Daniel Coyle, *The Culture Code: The Secrets of Highly Successful Groups* (New York: Bantam Books, 2018), 149-152.

78 James R. Deter. . .than R. Burris, "Can Your Employees Really Speak Freely?," *hbr.org*.

more aware of the kinds of questions you want to ask others, and how those inquiries can lead to new opportunities to strengthen relationships and increase your understanding about the world at large. And yes, it might involve being uncomfortable and even looking "stupid."

Polina Marinova, founder of The Profile, serves as another compelling example of a woman who is unabashed when it comes to this art form. Perhaps she has to be, because doing so is a critical skill required for her to excel in her job as a journalist.

Was she destined for this career path? Perhaps, as at just six years old she managed a diary that tracked and recorded interviews with friends and family. She remembers always having a fascination with gathering information and learning from other people. This skill in particular served her well upon the major life change of her immigration to the United States at eight years old.

In 2000, she and her parents migrated from Bulgaria to the city of Atlanta, Georgia. Polina would quickly be confronted with intense cultural shock and the need to rapidly learn a new language. When school started in the fall, although only finishing second grade in Bulgaria, she entered the fourth grade in the US because her math skills were well above average. But, for as skilled as her math was, her language skills were essentially nonexistent.

Ms. Jackson, her teacher at the time, saw that Polina was intensely curious and driven. During the entirety of her fourth-grade year, each night after school, Polina would go home with a children's book that her teacher provided her. At home, she would translate the books word for word using a dictionary. Over the course of the school year, her discipline and love for learning gave Polina a relatively easeful adjustment into the complexities of the English language.

Although the process of learning English was measurable for Polina, she struggled the most with the tacit cultural norms that rule American society. The cafeteria was one of her greatest summits to overcome. Unlike most of her classmates, she ate pizza with a fork and knife and was astoundingly confused at the concept of a corn dog. *"Who put a hot dog on a stick?"* She turned to observing fellow students as her weapon of choice to grasp the norms. By having awareness and a willingness to learn through examining others, she was able to both question and integrate the norms of American life into her own.

Nine years after stepping foot on American soil for the first time, Polina was accepted to the University of Georgia and graduated with a degree in journalism, with hopes that she could continue her passion for inquiry and make a career built on learning from others. However, in the same way that she questioned the dining etiquette in her elementary school's cafeteria, in college, she questioned the advice and wisdom that her professors preached as she journeyed through her undergraduate degree. A common theme she recalls was: "It doesn't matter where you live, as long as you have a job." Polina didn't quite agree, but nonetheless, graduated in 2013 and accepted an internship in Augusta, Georgia, even though her dream location, New York City, was over 700 miles away. For Polina, this internship paid the bills, but ultimately, she realized that it didn't make her feel fulfilled, and something needed to change. She craved an environment that stimulated her propensity for learning and development, so she set her mind on New York City.

Like we've learned from the Polynesian Wayfinders thousands of years before, Polina wasn't afraid to seek the unfamiliar and continually redefine her path. In 2014, she eventually landed her dream job at *Fortune Magazine* in New York City and more recently has pivoted again, leaving her position as an editor at *Fortune* to take on her role as founder and author of The Profile.

In finding success in her job at *Fortune*, she fell back on what she knew best: asking questions. "Really stupid questions," as she puts it. Coming full circle from her days of translating word for word in those toddler books from Ms. Jackson, in both journalism and life, Polina says, "I'm asking the questions that everybody else is thinking, and I'm not afraid to look dumb."

***

If asking questions seems to be so critical to facilitate pivots in life, then how can I improve upon this skill?

American novelist Thomas Berger says, "The art and science of asking questions is the source of all knowledge."[79] A few

---

79 Rama Satya Diwakar Grandhi, "The art and science of asking questions is the source of all knowledge!" *Medium*, March 4, 2018.

years ago on a Friday afternoon, a group of high schoolers broke up into small groups to practice this skill by generating as many questions as possible about Albert Camus' *The Plague*. The group was following instructions from Dan Rothstein, the cofounder of the Cambridge-based Right Question Institute, which is a nonprofit that seeks to help build people's question-asking skillsets.

By the end of the session, the high schoolers generated one hundred questions, but zero answers had been reached. In most any other circumstance, this outcome would be deemed a failure, but this was by design, as Rothstein's research is based on the assumption that questions are a tool that, if wielded correctly, can lead to new ideas and innovations rather than a simple, self-evident answer.[80] For generating *better* questions, perhaps we just need to have the confidence and ambition to ask *more* questions, even if we look dumb while doing so.

At the root of asking questions you'll find curiosity. In developing curiosity, Dalia Molokhia, author at Harvard Business Publishing, provides us a tactical approach. She mentions applying a beginner's mindset as a good place to start. Curiosity exists under the supposition that you don't have all the information, and it's this deprivation of information that leads you toward discovery, realizations, and pivots in life. With a beginner's mindset, we can begin to comprehend that, bound by our own inherent bias and preconceived notions, there's so much we don't know.

---

80   Leon Neyfakh, "Are we asking the right questions?" *Boston Globe*, May 20, 2012.

Unsurprisingly, she also mentions, "Ask questions, listen, and observe." For all the emphasis on asking questions, what can't be discredited is the ability for us to listen intently for the response. Stephen Covey sums it up perfectly through "Habit 5" in his book *7 Habits of Highly Effective People,* which states, "Seek first to understand before being understood."[81] Theoretically this makes perfect sense, but executing it is much harder. There's a significant tendency for ourselves to have our own voices and stories heard before we are willing to listen and accepts others'.

We've seen how Roshi Givechi and Polina exemplify this principle by being ceaselessly committed to the process of discovery, which Dalia says is one more way to develop curiosity. Whether it be Roshi listening intently to help IDEO solve its hardest problems, or Polina copying books word for word to learn the English language as a fourth grader, discovery and learning are intertwined with the concept of curiosity.

Lastly, Dalia mentions being inquisitive. This means seeking out perspectives different from your own. We all have confirmation bias. I've learned that one compelling idea to combat this bias is to consume media, whether that be podcasts or books, from people with vastly differing perspectives and assumptions from my own. Doing so creates friction in my mind, which can facilitate a great deal of learning.[82]

---

81   Stephen R. Covey, *The 7 Habit of Highly Effective People,* Simo...chuster Paperbacks, 247.

82   Dalia Molokhia, "The Importance Of Being Curious" *Harvard Business Publishing,* May 24, 2018.

As we've seen, questions are imperative to catalyzing change for ourselves, and underlying this ability is curiosity. George Loewenstein, a professor of economics and psychology at Carnegie Mellon University, proposed that curiosity, as alluded to before, is the feeling of deprivation we experience when we identify and focus on a gap in our knowledge.[83] But beyond the psychological view that Loewenstein supposes, it's worth noting that curiosity can be tied to our emotional states. It's an interesting insight because if we can control where and how we might feel most emotionally connected and interested, then that's precisely where our curiosity can blossom, and thus a pivot can be achieved.

You've likely experienced "peak curiosity" at a time where you were in a heightened emotional state due to a flood of new information and observations from an external stimulus. Maybe it was witnessing a beautiful sunrise in a remote location *(How did I arrive at this moment?)*, people-watching in a new country *(How does their culture and behavior differ from my own?)*, or listening to an expert present a compelling argument *(How can we end human trafficking?)*.

Around 1480, Leonardo Da Vinci arrived at a cave in the Tuscan countryside. He describes his own emotionally charged reaction as he approached the cavern:

Unable to resist my eager desire and wanting to see the great . . . of the various and strange shapes made by formative nature, and having wandered some distance among gloomy rocks, I

---

83 George Loewenstein, "The Psychology of Curiosity. . .eview and Reinterpretation," *American Psychological Association Psychological Bulletin*, vol. 116, 1994, accessed September 17, 2019.

came to the entrance of a great cavern, in front of which I stood
some time, astonished and unaware of such a thing. Bending
my back into an arch I rested my left hand on my knee and
held my right hand over my down-cast and contracted eye
brows: often bending first one way and then the other, to see
whether I could discover anything inside, and this being forbid-
den by the deep darkness within, and after having remained
there some time, two contrary emotions arose in me, fear
and desire—fear of the threatening dark cavern, desire to see
whether there were any marvelous thing within it.[84]

Da Vinci is known as one of the greatest inventors to have
ever lived. His journals are littered with iterations of sketches
and notes that depict everything from engineering contrap-
tions to horses' hooves and simple geometric shapes.[85]

It's easy to connect Da Vinci's intellectual capacity directly
to his ability to conceive ideas far ahead of his time like the
parachute, armored tank, or helicopter. However, it's important to understand that Da Vinci wasn't focused on generating
solutions. His ability to ask rather than pigeon-hole himself
with the burden of finding the perfect answer —like the students taking part in the Right Question Institute activity—
ultimately shaped his pervasive success.[86]

---

84 Frank Zöllner, "Leonardo da Vinci, 1452-151. . .he complete paintings and
    drawings," Collins Library Archives, 2003, accessed September 20, 2019.

85 Kate Sierzputowski, "Recently Digitized Journals Grant Visitors Access
    to Leonardo da Vinci's Detailed Engineering Schematics and Musings,"
    COLOSSAL, September 5, 2018.

86 Zat Rana, "The Underutilized Power of Questions," *Medium*, November 23,
    2017.

"Why is the sky blue?" is a question that could be answered within seconds from a Google search today. In fact, it led me to over five billion results in less than one second. But it was found in Da Vinci's journal, along with a plethora of others like, "Why does a dog sniff another dog's behind?" and "What makes a face beautiful?"[87]

Today, with technology as our enabler, we have the ability to ask almost any question at any time and find an answer relatively seamlessly and without much friction. Yet, what's troubling is that the rapid adoption and improvement of technologies like AI and machine learning provides us with systems that can predict not only what kind of question we might want to ask (*What restaurants are near me?*), but know what kind of answer we are seeking (*Here are vegetarian, eco-friendly restaurants with patio seating near you*). It's helpful of course, but when we are asking bigger questions (*Who should I vote for?*), the technologies already recognize what our biases are and the answers they display are in align with those biases, further confirming our own inherent predisposition and stifling us from discovery. In the case of attempting to utilize question-asking to discover new insights and lead me down new paths, this truth is rather concerning and serves, even more so than being fearful of asking questions themselves, as the greatest inhibitor in practicing this principle effectively.

In a time when answers weren't nearly as democratized and streamlined as they are currently, Da Vinci wasn't afraid

---

87 "Observing the journals of Leonardo da Vinci," *Journaling Habit*, March 25, 2017.

to ask questions that didn't have a seamlessly discoverable answer by way of an optimized search engine. He asked question upon question, many of which wouldn't be answered for centuries, and several of which would be labeled as "stupid" today.

There's probably never been a more relevant time in history for questioning to lead us to a new place or new learning opportunity. As we've seen with Roshi and Polina, *The Female Advantage* is exemplified by the power of asking effective questions and being transfixed on discovery as a process. In the age of the information economy, we are oftentimes bombarded by too much information and are left with having to learn *how* to sift through the plethora of material available to us, rather than go on a treasure hunt to find the information.

As Eric Reis, a Silicon Valley entrepreneur and author of *The Lean Startup*, puts it: "In the old economy, it was all about having the answers. But in today's dynamic, lean economy, it's more about asking the right questions. A more beautiful question is about figuring out how to ask and answer the questions that can lead to new opportunities and growth."[88]

For all of us today, there's plentiful opportunity to utilize our ability to ask questions as a powerful means to explore the unexplored, whether it be tangible concepts like a new job, a new city to move to, or even more abstract concepts like systemic racism or ancient art forms. By doing so, we will learn something new that could lead us down a new path.

---

88 "Eric Ries: "Figuring out how to ask,'. . .*ore Beautiful Question.*

When twentieth-century historian and philosopher Arnold Toynbee said, "Civilization is a movement and not a condition, a voyage and not a harbor," he probably didn't conceive the rate at which the world would be changing over the next few decades.[89] Yet, his quote endures today as a reminder that we aren't immovable or unchangeable. As simple as it seems, asking questions has allowed women individually to learn and develop, and collectively to reach new heights.

If civilization is both a movement and a voyage, perhaps it would do us some good to more critically question those points we are traveling both *toward* and *from*. Curiosity can help us get from point A to point B, but more importantly, it helps us question the As and the Bs themselves. In doing so, we become better equipped for asking the kinds of questions that might just lead us to new, undiscovered realizations.

---

89 "Arnold J. Toynbee Quotes," *All Author.*

CHAPTER 5

SHE'S INNOVATIVE

Failure is an option here. If things are not failing, you are not innovating enough.

-ELON MUSK

Most people know of Silicon Valley, the region in Northern California, as the hub for innovation and high-tech break-throughs. However, if you board a flight from San Francisco International Airport and fly 7,400 miles to the east, you'll land in what is called "Start-Up Nation," or what is also known as, "The Silicon Valley of the East."

Known by Israelis as the "Silicon Wadi" (wadi being the Hebrew word that translates to valley), Tel Aviv is a major metropolitan city in Israel that is credited for launching successful startups such as the navigation app Waze and the video and image editing application company Lightricks. Situated in the historically politically unstable region of the Middle East—sharing borders with Egypt, Saudi Arabia, Jordan, Syria, and Lebanon, along with struggling with its own longstanding Israeli-Palestinian conflict—it seems on paper that the systemic volatility existing in this region wouldn't be the best propellent for the intense innovation and passionate start-up culture that Tel Aviv and the nation of Israel at large exhibits. However, Israel has more venture capital dollars per capita and more startups per capita than any other country in the world.

The structure of Israeli's democratic government and capitalistic society is most certainly a factor in the success of innovation that Israel has seen historically, however, an Israeli's cultural identity plays a critical role here as well. Within this deep-rooted cultural identity, we'll discover the two major factors for innovation, and then we'll apply these factors to the stories of women later in this chapter.

It all begins with the Hebrew language itself, which has specific words that embody the essence of this innovative culture. The word *combina* for example, is the internalized belief of an Israeli that affects his or her actions and propensity toward risk-taking and thus innovation.

Let's say there's an Israeli college student who has a dream to attend a music festival in London. Unfortunately, she doesn't have the funds to purchase a plane ticket to get there. When she's walking to class one day, she notices a poster for a sustainability conference happening in London the week before the music festival. She restructures (or perhaps the better word is, embellishes) her resume to depict her widespread involvement in environmental initiatives all over campus and in the local Tel Aviv community, none of which she's actually involved in. She writes a compelling essay about her passion to eliminate her carbon footprint and to live sustainably in the name of environmentalism.

With all of her credentials, she receives an invitation to attend the conference, which includes the cost of the plane ticket that she originally couldn't afford herself. In London, she attends the entirety of the conference, but once it's over, she extends her trip in order to fulfil her dream of attending the music festival.

Upon arrival back to Israel, her friends and family meet her at the airport with signs and are cheering loudly. *Why?* She's being praised because of her ingenuity and creativity in living out the principle of *combina* in its entirety.

Further regarding innovative thought, Israelis have another word that helps describe their attitudes toward failure. *Fahida* is a slang term that Israelis use to make light of failure and disappointment. If an Israeli embarrasses herself by volunteering to play an instrument in front of a crowd when she really has no idea how to play it, her friends would encourage her to keep trying for the sake of *fahida*.

The practice of these values has real world implications. A few years ago, Dr. Ben Reis, current director at Harvard Medical School, was asked to help his friends at an Israeli start-up with hiring a new employee. That day, the first person Dr. Reis interviewed didn't have one positive thing to say about his past experiences. The candidate's background included having previously been at three start-ups that failed, so on paper and in the interview, he seemed like a real loser.

However, the other candidates Dr. Reis interviewed were significantly more promising, with more experience at well-established and successful companies. At the end of the day, when it was time to deliberate on who would be hired, one of Dr. Reis friends, a founder at the start-up said, "The first guy. It's obvious." Perplexed, Dr. Reis responded with, "Yeah, the first guy sucked."

At that, his friends and the team at the start-up opposed him, explaining that the first candidate was precisely the one they would, in fact, be hiring. The basis of this decision is best summed up by the founder's opinions: "We're in a start-up. We have chaos every day and a crisis every few months. That other candidate at Google only has to worry about his iced coffee or avocado toast. This guy's a fighter. That's who we need."

It's precisely this mentality that best expresses Israel's culture of innovation and why they are so successful at it. It's also the reason that other countries have started to adopt these values for themselves. There's power in *combina* and *fahida*.

South Korea, a society where education is highly valued, is paying large amounts of money for their children to study Jewish texts, which helps them learn to think more critically. The discussion and analysis of Jewish texts, which has been expressed in the Israeli culture for thousands of years, essentially teaches someone how to effectively argue and converse.

It turns out, this isn't a skill that is democratized across every culture nowadays. Where the South Korean cultures emphasizes memorization and repetition, they now see a shift toward learning that is more Socratic and discursive in nature as inspired from the Israeli culture, which is heavily influenced with Jewish ethnic norms, values, and religious practices. It seems that reading, discussing, and debating Jewish texts can teach all people how to be real-world problem solvers.[90]

The value placed on living out *combina*, which specifically translates to, "create something from nothing," or, "working your way around something to get what you want," is a primary reason for Israel's sustained innovative success. Although I need to note that "Israeli" and "Jew" aren't perfectly substitutable terms, perhaps this ability to practice ingenuity (*combina*), and to not fear failure (*fahida*) are main contributors to the fact that, although Jews make up less than 0.2 percent of the world population, they account for 23 percent of Nobel Prize winners.

As we've seen, the Israelis have a keen appreciation of failure imbedded in their cultural identity which, perhaps counterintuitively, is what has spurred their technological and educational successes. Of course, we could debate the ethics of embellishing a resume like the student in the example above, but from a more theoretical point of view, the grounds by which she practices innovation and met her goal to attend the music festival were based on her choice to get creative (*combina*) and to be unafraid of failing (*fahida*).

***

---

90   Tim Alper, "Talmud-inspired learning craze sweeps South Korea," *Jewish Telegraphic Agency,* January 14, 2019.

Although Israel seems to embody the epitome of these values, they are still evident in women from all around the world, and Sandy Lerner is one such woman who meets both of these criteria for practicing innovation. From her story, we can see how doing so can lead us to change different aspects of our lives and bring us down newfound paths.

It was during her childhood in the 60s, on her aunt's cattle ranch in the California Sierras, where she first practiced her entrepreneurial aptitude. At the age of nine, she purchased her very own steer, then sold it two years later, and then bought two more steer with the profit she had made. Through repeating this process, she eventually accumulated a herd of thirty cattle and used the income she generated from them to pay for her undergraduate degree at California State University-Chico.

Shortly after graduating, in 1975, she began a master's program at Claremont College. It was there that Sandy stumbled across the college's computer lab. She began utilizing the lab to conduct comparative political studies research. She recalls her days in the lab, where the intersection of her political studies research with computer analysis was unheard of at the time and says she remembers that, "People left you alone because they thought you were weird, and nobody knew anything about what you were doing."

After graduating from Claremont, she made her way to Stanford University's graduate program for statistics and computer science. It was here that she met and dated Leonard Bosack, a fellow computer engineer, and they married in 1980. Leonard and Sandy both found jobs on Stanford's campus, but there was one problem for this newly married couple: although they worked on the same campus, they were separated by 500 yards each day in their prospective office buildings. This distance, although seemingly insignificant, is what caused Sandy to *get creative* about how she could better transfer computer data between her and her husband and additionally, simply communicate with him without having to complete the five-minute walk over to the computer science department.

What ultimately developed from this pain point was a solution that personally solved Sandy and Leonard's communication constraint, but more so, created a network linking all of Stanford's five thousand computers. This innovation had incredibly far reaching implications, and thus had a largely positive, *lottery-type* change potential for Sandy. However, although their concept was cutting edge and unprecedented at the time, venture capitalists claimed it wasn't an idea they could monetize.

Nonetheless, Sandy, *refused to live in fear of failure*, and in 1984, quit her job at Stanford in the name of her and Leonard's business idea. Soon after, Cisco, a computer networking company, was born. However, after new management began to take over in the late 80s, Sandy found herself ousted by the CEO.

Sandy exhibited innovation from the start. She was able to solve her personal problem of communication on Stanford's campus and then expand that on a greater scale. Even when the top-dog venture capital firms told her the idea would fail, she still had the guts to quit her job and pursue her dream.

When Cisco went public in 1990, Sandy and Leonard found themselves with a very tangible *lottery-type* change: $85 million worth of Cisco stock.

What would she do now?

The interesting thing about innovation is that it can be iterated upon. Within the practice of innovation, one can explore various possibilities and pivots. As Steve Jobs puts it, "Innovation is the ability to see change as an opportunity—not a threat."[91]

Maybe it would have made the most sense for Sandy to stick to her computer skills and launch another network-type company. However, she did something that seems rather random. She launched a cosmetics company. The same thought process of, "I have a problem, I want to solve it," that she used on Stanford's campus years before had now brought her to this vastly new territory.

Within the beauty industry, Sandy refused to accept the stereotypical pinks and reds used profusely in nail polishes and lipsticks at the time. So, she decided to create a more iconoclastic and alternative brand, creating products with colors that tended toward the blue-green-purple-black spectrum, with names such as "Bruise," "Smog," and "Roach." She even launched a maverick marketing campaign with the tag line, "Does Pink Make You Puke?"

---

91 "Innovation is the ability to see change as an opportunity—no. . .hreat," *azquotes.com.*

Perhaps you've heard of the makeup company Sandy started. Urban Decay has grown to be one of the most popular makeup brands today, and it all began with a woman who exemplified Israeli inputs to innovation, getting creative and not being afraid to fail.[92]

***

So far, we've learned about innovation through the Israeli culture and have seen how it was executed from a female lens in Sandy's story, which lead her to experience the stark change of computer networker to cosmetics guru. The fascinating thing about innovation is that you can practice it in so many ways and in basically any context. It's not something that is only bound to the business world or confined within the walls of a technology conference. Innovation can be introduced into our personal lives, helping us solve relational problems and think critically within the contexts of our communities. As readily available as this principle is to each of us, at the same time, innovation can have incredibly far-reaching implications.

Ayanna Howard is another woman who knows plenty about this, as she's stretched the idea of innovation and humanistic approach in problem-solving to a place over one hundred million miles away. She wasn't always working on engineering rovers for Mars, but she always had a knack for thinking outside the box and generating change by bringing diverse viewpoints and ideas to the table through a human-centered approach to problem-solving. From her story, we can see the

---

92 "Sandy Lerner Biography," *Encyclopedia of World Biography*.

Israeli components of innovation in action and take away our own ideas for how we can practice innovation in any part of our lives.

Ayanna's interest in robotics first began as a child when she was given a computer, solder kit, and programming knowledge from her father. As a third grader in the early 80s, she set out with the lofty goal of building the first bionic woman. Today, Dr. Ayanna Howard is a roboticist, co-founder of a technology company, and the endowed chair at the School of Interactive Computing at Georgia Tech.[93]

Those three items that she had at her disposal growing up were not the only distinguishing input factors to her success. The other essential asset in the equation was support and space to fail from her father, who was an engineer himself. From very early on, Ayanna had the freedom to venture into unconventional space and assumed the principle that anything she broke was excused, so long as she could put it back together. As a young girl, her home became a playground for inventing that allowed her to *get creative*. Her father's support provided her with *freedom to fail*. As we'll see, both of these components catalyzed her innovative successes.

During her childhood, even with her radically ambitious goals, Ayanna didn't feel like she was going "against the grain" per se. As much as she was interested in building robots, she always maintained an amicable nature. She remembers her naturally helpful and human-centric nature growing up,

---

93 "Ayanna MacCalla Howard," *Georgia Tech School of Electrical and Computer Engineering Faculty Staff Directory.*

recalling, "If I saw people having a hard time, I'm like, 'Hey I can help!' I was always a social girl, I grew up [believing] that you make friends everywhere."

This ability for Ayanna to connect with others provided her a sense of meaning and purpose early on in her life that has since perpetuated into finding meaning and purpose in her professional career as an innovator. As Michael Dell, CEO of Dell Technologies says, "Collaboration equals innovation."[94]

Yet, from a statistical standpoint today as an African American woman, Ayanna is a maverick. In STEM, African American women make up less than 13 percent of female master's degree recipients, less than 1 percent of women with doctoral degrees, and less than 1 percent of women employed as scientists or engineers.[95] Nonetheless, she continued to reach the major milestones of education, ultimately receiving her PhD in Electrical Engineering from the University of Southern California in 1994.

It was shortly after receiving her PhD that she started her dream job at NASA, where she began working in the Jet Propulsion Laboratory as a senior robotics researcher. She would work there for the next ten years, paving the way for NASA's robotics research for years to come.

During her time at NASA, she served as principal investigator of the Safe Rover Navigation task, which is an initiative

---

94 Asad Meah, "35 Inspirational Michael Dell Quotes on Success," *Awakening the Greatness Within.*

95 Olivia A. Scriven, PhD, "Why So Few? African American Women in STEM—Part II: By the Numbers," *Scientista*, May 7, 2013.

that enables rovers to traverse on challenging terrains such as Mars.[96] It seems as though a planet so far away, with no human life, wouldn't be the best test grounds for this "human-centered approach" to innovation that Ayanna proposed. But, for as different as robots and a Martian landscape may seem to be compared to us humans here on earth, she nonetheless looked at human behavior itself to drive the project's success.

Specifically, in an effort to think innovatively, she thought about what humans would do in order to guide what the robots' behavior would be. The goal here is that the rover on Mars would be able to react in the same way that a human navigating the terrain on Mars would. *How would a human effectively traverse this landscape?* Okay, let's program the robot similarly. Like an autonomous vehicle, the robot would be able to successfully navigate various terrains and make decisions such as where it should land and how it should navigate from point A to point B. The simple and small, *lollipop-type* ways of positively changing the way her team thought about rovers traversing on Mars lead to substantial outcomes as the application that the team built would help future missions to Mars decide on optimal landing sites.

What Ayanna and her team at NASA were doing in the early 2000s is very similar to the concept of design-thinking today, which is an approach to innovation that can be used by anyone under any condition. However, when she was working on her rovers for Mars, design-thinking and this

---

96 Meredith Rizzo, "Being Different Helpe. . .ASA Roboticist Achieve Her Dream," *NPR*, December 19, 2017.

human-ocentered approach to innovation were a large shift in thought from the way problems had been solved before. Ayanna wasn't afraid to bring new ideas to the table in order to bring about the best changes possible to guarantee the projects' success.

Regarding design thinking, IDEO (the same organization mentioned in Chapter 4 with Roshi Givechi's story) is the originator of many design-thinking concepts and frameworks today. Particularly, one of their signature frameworks to problem-solving is: empathize, define, ideate, prototype, and then test. This framework has more than just business and scientific applications, and can help us even in the personal inquiry and daily tasks we take part in.

To empathize, one might ask, "What are your thoughts on sending a rover to Mars?" or, "What is important to you when we build the rover?" In asking these questions, we become better equipped to best meet the needs of the people involved in the project or who personally encounter the problem we are trying to solve.

With "define," we can get a more detailed scope on the question we are asking in order to ensure we arrive at the best possible answer. Let's say, like Ayanna, we are trying to ascertain the constraints of landing a rover on Mars. We might ask, "Why would we choose one locale over another?" or, "What various atmospheric conditions might we encounter during landing?"

After that is "ideate." Given what we now know about what various stakeholders value from empathizing with them and defining the scope of the question itself, we can now think of ideas to suggest. The idea here is that no potential solution is discredited. Sometimes it's those weird, quirky solutions that could actually be the most effective.

After that is "prototype," which is building out the idea with concrete examples. This might be creating the product, iterating on it, and creating a beta version of the product or rough iteration. Perhaps before we build out a complete rover for Mars, we design several concepts and then pick the best parts from each to assemble into the final creation.

The last step is "test." User acceptance testing, conducting surveys, or gathering qualitative data are all examples of testing. In our case, before landing the rover on Mars, we might want to put it through some of Earth's most rugged terrain, to validate its effectiveness. Within this framework, what's important to note is that these steps don't necessarily have to be properly recorded in a formalized sense, but just keeping the framework in mind can help you think more creatively about solving problems you face on a daily basis in a more human-centric way, which could lead to new insights and innovations that catalyze change either internally or externally. Using this framework doesn't have to be applied to something as large-scale as Martian missions. It could be something as simple as asking "How can I better communicate with my team at work?" or "What's the best way to structure my morning routine?"

Of course, Ayanna wasn't exactly utilizing IDEO's framework during her time at NASA, but the essence is there, and now you can consider it the next time you are problem-solving.

The main idea in this case is that the design-thinking process is iterative. Similar to how Ayanna grew up with the two components to innovation at her disposal (the space to practice creativity as well as the freedom to fail), creative thought processes and failure are embraced and not frowned upon as you move through this framework. For those trying to be more innovative, this concept can be particularly difficult (who likes failing?), but remarkably beneficial. It can help us all think of things in a more creative and playful way and help bring new ideas and different perspectives to solving problems and generating change for ourselves or the world at large.

After her time at NASA, where Ayanna brought about changes in thought and execution for her team, she began work as a professor at Georgia Institute of Technology, where she currently serves as chair to the school's College of Computing. With her background in innovative problem-solving, she was curious to deepen her understanding about the relationship between robots and humans, so she ran an experiment that went like this:

Imagine you're in a room alone taking part in a research study you think is about answering some questions about your thoughts on robots. Suddenly, the fire alarm starts blaring. You stand up, open the door, and are met with smoke. You look around to analyze your surroundings, and then you notice a robot, fashioned with emergency labels, flashing its lights at you, beckoning you to join it on its journey to guiding you to safety. However, you notice the emergency exit sign is in the *opposite direction* that the robot is leading you in.

Would you trust the robot and follow it?

If you were like the vast majority of the research participants, you followed the robot. Even if the robot brought you to a dark, empty room, or if the robot was spinning mindlessly in circles, you still decided to follow it. The takeaway from this experiment is that as humans, we all have a preconceived inclination to trust the systems in our societies. Ironically, we often don't think innovatively ourselves when it comes to our interactions with such advanced innovations.[97]

How can I be innovative and how will that change the way I interpret things?

We've touched on how Ayanna practiced innovation, and how the application of IDEO's framework can help drive innovation in our lives. Nonetheless, it can be hard, especially when our brains have a natural tendency to go on autopilot so often, as we've seen in Ayanna's research. Nobel Prize-winning psychologist Daniel Kahneman understands this propensity of the brain to "take a back seat" when he says, "Our comforting conviction that the world makes sense rests on a secure foundation: our almost unlimited ability to ignore our ignorance."[98]

Critical thinking is one way to push ourselves beyond our own ignorance and acceptance of what's going on around us, and it can catalyze innovations and meaningful insights in

---

97 Ayanna Howard, "Why We Need to Build Robots We Can Trust," *TED*, November 2018.

98 Sims Wyeth, "20 Wise, Humbling Quotes fro. . .obel Prize Winning Psychologist," *Inc.*, January 21, 2016.

our lives. Critical thinking is one of the best tools to utilize when questioning our assumptions, whether it be robots or other systems or norms under which we function as human beings. Helen Lee Bouygues, President of the Reboot Foundation on Critical Thinking has a simple, three-part model to help people improve upon their critical thinking acumen: 1. Question assumptions, 2. Reason through logic, and 3. Diversify thought.[99]

For questioning assumptions, the more important objective would be to figure out *when* to question the assumptions. By doing so, you can realize alternatives. In the case of Ayanna's research participants, when the stakes are high, it is a particularly critical time to quickly question the assumptions and beliefs that you are functioning under in order to make the best decision given the information you have at that moment. *Should I follow the robot?*

For reasoning through logic, Aristotle, one of the most notable logicians, has a useful concept called the Golden Mean, which is the idea that a desirable middle ground exists between the two extremes of deficiency and excess. Typically applied to morality, for example, the middle ground between indecisiveness and impulsiveness is self-control, this reasoning can be exercised with regard to the participants in the study who chose to trust the robot. A middle ground of trusting both the robot and the emergency sign exists, if the participant were to give the robot a chance to prove its validity (i.e., *Will the robot lead me in the direction of the*

---

99   Helen Lee Bouygues, "3 Simple Habits to Improve Your Critical Thinking," *Harvard Business Review,* May 6, 2019.

emergency exit?). The moment the robot opposes the exit sign would be a great time to reason through the logic of trusting the robot and formulate an alternate plan if the robot is opposing our logic.

Diversifying thought is a bank that can be invested in from various experiences. It is human nature to align our social relationships around those with similar views. What this contributes to is groupthink, or the absence of a person to contribute ideas that are different than those around them. One way to practice diversifying thought is to seek out people who have opposing views to your own, whether that be political, economic, or religious views. This will force you to think about things from a different perspective. Ayanna didn't run her experiment with a group, but a fair hypothesis would be if she did, the collective group would follow the robot. Diversifying thought allows us to learn more from others but also helps us learn how to effectively verbalize our opposing viewpoints. In the case of life or death in a fire, verbalizing your thoughts regarding the appropriate exit strategy would be imperative.

For Ayanna, diversifying thought was one of the main factors that has perpetuated her success throughout her career in the execution of innovation, allowing her to bring different ideas and values to her team. It's not exactly about the visible and surface level things such as where you grew up or where you're from, or how much money your parents had. For Ayanna, diversifying thought really comes down to having something a little different to bring to the table. Whether it be a divergent insight or a novel idea, it's often the introduction of creative concepts, like design-thinking or critical thinking, that significantly contribute to positive changes within problem solving and innovation.

Much like how humans on Mars will become just the "tip of the iceberg" of space exploration, Ayanna's external appearance and prior experiences are only just the "tip of the iceberg" for defining diversity for herself. Ultimately, it's her ability to think of things a little differently that has perpetuated her success when exploring new ideas and solving difficult problems throughout her career.

From her work with robots on Mars and her research on humans' propensity for trusting robots, to her current work with developing robots that help engage children in STEM through her company Zyrobotics, there's a lot left unanswered about the trajectory of innovation for Ayanna and the world at large. Whether it be traversing Martian landscapes or wayfinding to an emergency exit, most can agree that innovation, and the changes that occur from it, are what will determine humanity's success in the future.

As we've seen through the examples of Sandy Lerner and Ayanna Howard, trailblazers like them serve as exemplary embodiments of *The Female Advantage* for practicing innovation. These women are strong utilizers of this principle and their stories reveal the benefits in practicing innovation, as using this principle led each of them to new ideas and pivots, both large and small, in their lives. Li Keqiang, China's head of government, echoes this notion when he says, "Changes call for innovation, and innovation leads to progress."[100] Along the same vein as Keqiang, and from what we've learned from the stories of the women above, it's clear that practicing innovation can precipitate personal pivots in our lives, as well as helps us rumble through problem-solving for the external fluctuations we will indeterminably face throughout our lives.

---

100 "30 of Our Favorite Quotes On Innovation," *workspace.digital.*

CHAPTER 6

SHE BELIEVES
IN HERSELF

———

*Faith is the art of holding on to things in spite of your changing
moods and circumstances.*

- C.S. LEWIS

"We have to change our behaviors before it's too late."

At just sixteen years old, Delaney stepped onto the TEDx
stage in Miami, Florida, and made the above statement with
regard to the topic of climate change and rising sea levels. At
just 5'2", she boldly raised her hand well over her head in an
effort to describe where the sea levels would be within the
next one hundred years. Based off of the scientific models,
Delaney would be entirely submerged.

If nothing is done today, the effects of rising sea levels will
have the most significant impact on the generations beyond
Delaney, with the bulk of the predicted damage occurring

well after she is no longer alive. One could project this reality into thinking that because it doesn't affect her personally right now, it doesn't matter. However, Delaney is incredibly passionate about creating a change today that will make a difference for generations in the future.

Now twenty years old, Delaney is a current student at University of Miami's Rosensteil School of Marine and Atmospheric Science. As a student, she has worked tirelessly to gain the respect of, or simply just the face time with, government officials in her local community and at the national level to raise awareness for environmentalism, and specifically, the rising sea waters right in the familiarity of her backyard.

Having grown up on No Name Key, a 1,000-acre island with forty-three solar-powered homes imbedded seamlessly into nature, at a young age, Delaney took a keen interest at how humans coexist within the ecosystems they live in. Today, she's the founder of the Sink or Swim Project, and has successfully brought millions in funding toward the preservation of the coastline of Miami, as well as petitioned and rallied for national governmental leaders to take a larger stance on sustainability in the entirety of the United States.

It wasn't necessarily simple for her to ignite the change she desired. In 2015, she was shocked to learn that her hometown in Miami-Dade County, which had a $7 billion budget, was allocating zero dollars toward climate change efforts. In fact, the 2016 budget proposal, a document that is almost one thousand pages long, mentioned climate change just once.

Delaney knew she needed to get policy makers on board to remediate this proposal, so she went to the county commission meeting and spoke in front of the mayor, demanding that he revise the budget. She ambitiously requested a *lottery-type* change: an allocation of $1 million toward the cause.

Because of her efforts, the mayor agreed to apportion $300,000 toward the rising sea levels and created a position for the county's first ever chief sustainability officer. However, Delaney is transparent enough to say that neither $300,000 or $1,000,000 is enough, but she reminds us that this is only the starting place, and that even if small in scale, igniting some small, *lollipop-type* positive change is better than no positive change at all.

When speaking with Delaney, it is blatantly apparent that she has a strong sense of urgency to do something *now*. For inherently systemic problems like climate change, it's often easy to feel discouraged that efforts of bettering the world— for example, bypassing the intake of meat for one meal a day, or say, taking public transportation to reduce the total output of gas emissions— don't make *enough* of a difference or generate *enough* change. Delaney empathizes: "It's hard to feel discouraged, because this is such a large issue and it almost feels like you can't do enough. But everything you consciously do to help is helping in a way. Even if it doesn't seem like much, if everyone were to start doing these things, then it would make a massive impact."

The power of Delaney's story lies in the cornerstone of self-belief. She refused to use her age or inexperience as an excuse to stop her from achieving what she hoped to. On her path to helping the environment, she never doubted that her efforts would be impactful and her belief in her own ability to make an impact remained unwavering, even when tackling such a large-scale, multi-dimensional problem like climate change.

***

How much of a difference can belief really make?

"If 'I believe I can fly,' as the 1996 song by R. Kelly goes, I won't actually fly. . ."[101]

There's no debate there. Belief in yourself can only go so far in actualizing some kind of change. There is an upper limit.

Delaney's story gives us a compelling view on the changes we can actualize from practicing this principle for ourselves. But maybe you aren't compelled to go to your local government to demand some kind of policy change that will impact the community for years to come. Nonetheless, the components of what underlies her actions can still be relevant to all of us.

Depending on your personal background and current environment, among countless other factors, belief most likely looks very different for you. Yet for everyone, it begins with yourself. Belief begins when the idea of achieving something is first conceived in your mind and then executed in the form of tangible actions. We've seen this with how Delaney herself

---

101 Stacy Lambe, *Space Jam* 20 Years Later: How "I Believ. . .an Fly" Transformed R. Kelly's Career, *etonline.com*, November 15, 2016.

had executed her own self-belief in the form of demanding change within her community.

Belief isn't the age-old cliché, "seeing is believing," but instead, "achieving is believing." And in order to persist in the direction of achieving anything, the most rudimentary baseline requirement is to first and foremost, as professional tennis player Venus Williams puts it, "Believe in yourself, when no one else does, (and) that makes you a winner right there."[102]

Maybe it still sounds too abstract or theoretical. I think there's no better way to sum up the essence of belief than from this quote by Teddy Roosevelt:

"It is not the critic who counts; not the man who points out how the strong man stumbles, or where the doer of deeds could have done them better. The credit belongs to the man who is actually in the arena, whose face is marred by dust and sweat and blood; who strives valiantly; who errs who comes short again and again, because there is no effort without error and shortcoming; but who does actually strive to do the deeds; who knows great enthusiasms, the great devotions; who spends himself in a worthy cause; who at the best knows in the end the triumph of high achievement, and who at the worst, if he fails, at least fails while daring greatly, so that his place shall never be with those cold and timid souls who neither know victory nor defeat."[103]

---

102 "Top 20 Serena Williams Quotes to Inspire You to Rise Up and Win," *Goalcast*, August 8, 2017.

103 Christen Duxbury, "It Is Not the Critic Who Counts," *Theodore Roosevelt Conservation Partnership*, January 18, 2011.

In middle school, I absolutely loved playing dodgeball during gym class, and because of my competitive nature, I would take it rather seriously. While other girls clung to the back of the walls of the gymnasium, when the gym teacher blew his whistle, I raced forward at full force to the dodgeballs in the center of the gym.

I retrieved those dodgeballs as fast as I could and would then back away, scoping out the current situation. Sometimes, during these first moments, as I attempted to dodge those first few balls thrown my way, someone would very easily hit me as I made a futile attempt at running away. Other times, I would perhaps hit a classmate or two successfully before succumbing to my own demise.

One time though, I recall being the last one standing on my team. Both fear and excitement arose within me as my fight or flight response was enabled. I found myself flooded with newfound motivation from my team cheering me on from the sideline. *I can do this.* The other team still had a few others in the game, and as I fiercely battled with all of my ability, fruitlessly throwing dodgeballs and dodging the ones flying toward my tiring body, for as much effort as I could produce, it was not enough. I lost.

Teddy Roosevelt also said, "It is hard to fail, but it is worse never to have tried."[104]

---

104 Steve Agyei, "It is hard to fail, but it is worse never to have tried to succeed.," *medium.com*, December 17, 2015.

I was fearlessly in the arena. I refused to be, "those cold and timid souls" clinging to the walls in fear of being hit. Although at the time I was playing against some fierce competition with considerably more athletic talent than myself and knew fully well that I probably wouldn't be the last participant standing, I still *opted into the arena*. The arena isn't always a pretty place to be or even the most comfortable for that matter, but there's something enticing about it. The arena brings out your best.

When it comes to your own arena, the first step is the choice to opt in. Belief in oneself is undoubtedly the crux to stepping into the complexities and risks associated with the arena. Delaney herself, among countless other women, are in their own arenas. If we look critically at her story, we can find two main factors to her own self-belief: A focus on her strengths and abilities, and the environment she functioned within. Delaney used her passion and voice to demand change and discovered the political arena to be the best space for her to use her skills to facilitate the change she was seeking.

Applied to my personal gym class experience, I utilized my ability (although not of extreme talent), and then applied that within a culture (middle school gym class) that brought out my greatest efforts. What's important here is that we can apply these two components of self-belief to our own lives to help us make conscious pivots or help us to better navigate the environmental changes we may have little control over.

Given these components to believing in oneself, how might we make a conscious pivot toward practicing these two factors in our own lives?

We all have abilities and gifts. One of the best things we can do to cultivate self-belief is to explore our strengths and learn how to most effectively play to them. A growing body of research supports the claim that focusing on our strengths has various benefits, such as being more energized and feeling happier.[105] I hope you can think of many times when playing to your strengths has benefitted you greatly. Whether that be teaching someone how to play your favorite instrument or using your attention to detail to find a spelling error in a contract for your job, there's no shortage of opportunities to use your strengths to your advantage. Understanding exactly what your strengths are and what value you can add in various environments is the first place to start.

If you're not quite sure what your strengths are exactly, start by asking coworkers and close friends. You could even create an anonymous survey so the respondents would feel comfortable with being wholly honest. You could also self-inquire. Most of the time, humans tend to take part in activities they are good at or have skill in. Think about the parts of your life that make you feel the most talented or most impactful. At this intersection you can best see your strengths on display, and precisely where you can generate change for yourself.

With our own individual abilities in mind, now we can explore environments where they are maximized. From my story, it was my strength of being competitive that was able to be displayed and refined through the game of dodgeball.

---

105 Megan Dalla-Camina, "Are You Playing to Your Strengths at Work?" *Psychology Today*, November 11, 2018.

For Delaney, is was her expression of her passion for the environment to the right people: policymakers and change agents in her local community.

For as valuable as our abilities are in and of themselves, if we can't practice them in an environment that nurtures and further develops them, then they aren't going to improve and grow, and thus less change will be actualized. In an exaggerated example, let's say you're the best cook in the world. Your life is exclusively dedicated to this craft. The job market is rough, and you find yourself with a new job as a line cook in a federal prison. You spend your days scooping beans out of a can and buttering bread. This job would not be conducive to your ability to demonstrate your full abilities as a talented chef. In other words, it's not the *right environment* for your strengths to be utilized to their greatest potential.

For each of us trying to transcend environments that might not allow us to express our strengths to their full potential, what could be useful here is conducting an "occupation audit" and critically analyzing your job and the work you do against your own strengths. *Is the environment nurturing my skills or hindering them? Are my coworkers bringing out my best, (and me, theirs)?* In this evaluation you are better equipped to objectively see how you can best create impact. All of this discussion on strengths and the environment under which they're illuminated is so important because ultimately these inputs, as I've mentioned and we'll discover in another female example below, are instrumental in navigating change effectively and creating change for ourselves.

***

We can further explore the concept of belief from the way it's related to the idea of self-efficacy.

Self-efficacy is a concept synonymous with the idea of believing in oneself. Research has shown that a high level of self-efficacy can contribute to a person being more likely to achieve his or her goals. Psychologist Albert Bandura developed his own theory based off of the concept, which he defines as, "The belief in one's capabilities to organize and execute the sources of action required to manage prospective situations." Bandura hypothesized that self-efficacy, or belief in oneself, is a major factor in our abilities to perceive different situations and determine effective responses.[106]

Kristin Fleschner serves as a powerful example of a woman who practices self-efficacy on a daily basis. Today, as an athlete, lawyer, and advocate for marginalized groups, she's consulting and engaging with companies on leadership, accessibility, and diversity and inclusion, as well as preparing for the upcoming para-Olympic Games tryouts and unequivocally leaning on her own belief in her abilities in order to do so successfully.

In the eighth grade, Kristin was diagnosed with type 1 diabetes. However, she never let that stop her. Growing up, her parents provided the perfect culture of support and rigor, and wanted Kristin to continue achieving her goals, refusing to see the disease as something that could stop her. To empower Kristin as a young woman, her parents signed her up for a

---

106 Kendra Cherry, "Quotes from Albert Bandura on His Theories," *verywellmind.com*, May 5, 2020.

summer camp that included a weekend bike trip. However, exercise for those with type 1 diabetes can oftentimes be challenging, as blood sugar can get either too high or too low, resulting in hyperglycemia, with symptoms including extreme thirst, nausea, or hypoglycemia, with symptoms including racing pulse, cold sweats, or restlessness.

With symptoms so severe, it might make sense for Kristin's parents to want to protect her from the risks involved with exercising as a diabetic. However, her parents sought to support her. At that camp, being on the bike and riding with her dad provided her an outlet of freedom to be in her own world, even if just for a few hours, away from the stresses and anxieties that a typical young girl, particularly one with diabetes, faces. Years later, she still craves that sense of freedom and allows it to propel her forward, even as she would begin to face further challenges.

Research from the Wilmer Eye Institute at John Hopkins University reveals that out of all possible ailments one could have, most Americans believe loss of vision to be the worst ailment that could happen to them, ranking above losing a limb, loss of hearing or speech, and loss of memory. For Kristin, this would soon become a reality, but for her, this type of change wasn't as *life-threatening* as it might seem to be as depicted by most Americans in the study.[107]

Her vision loss began in 2007, when she underwent a pancreas transplant due to complications with her diabetes.

---

107 Jane E. Brody, "The Worst That Could Happen? Going Blind, People Say," February 20, 2015, *nytimes.com*.

Immediately after the pancreas transplant surgery, she noticed she wasn't able to read the small text on a newspaper. The doctors found a bit of swelling in her eyes, but ultimately, they weren't entirely sure what was going on. The years following her transplant were met with various procedures consisting of eye surgeries, injections, and various prescription drugs in an attempt to ameliorate Kristin's worsening sight. However, her sight continued to deteriorate more and more, until a day came when, while she was completing the simple task of her daily morning routine, she realized her vision might be beyond repair.

Before this point, her vision had been slowly regressing, but not enough for her or her doctors to understand the severity of what was happening. As she leaned in toward the mirror to put on eyeliner, she became acutely aware of how badly she was struggling to do so. In that moment, she recognized that her lack of sight was affecting her in the fundamentally personal way of interfering in something as mundane as a morning routine. Her mind raced as she began to question how she could continue to function as a "normal" human being if she struggled to successfully complete even the most basic of tasks.

It almost goes without saying that for many women, self-care provides a sense of value and serves as an expression for themselves. A typical day might start with the customary ritual of waking up each morning, brushing her teeth, washing her face, and putting on some form of makeup. This ritual, like many of the patterns of human life, is something that is easily taken for granted because it is so embedded into our patterns of life that it's almost automatic. Have you ever questioned whether or not you brushed your teeth moments after you actually did so? That's what I'm getting at here. Research points to these patterns as being almost ritualistic, which provided people a sense of control in their lives. For Kristin, this morning ritual was taken away.[108] This change, which appears on the surface to be largely negative in nature, *life-threatening* type as stated above, would provide her with new opportunities to practice a deep level of self-belief and would lead her to positive outcomes for herself and other disabled people as well.

As mentioned, Kristin's transition to losing her vision was not immediate, but was also not gradual. In the midst of this transition, she began the process of adapting to this "new normal" in her daily life. She needed to change various aspects of her daily routine and rituals, like having to adjust the way she picked out her clothing from her closet or change the way she navigated the streets as a pedestrian through rush hour traffic.

Nonetheless, what didn't change was her belief in her abilities to achieve her goals. Instead of sitting back and lamenting her impending loss, she continued to plow forward, asking herself if her goals actually needed significant adjustment or if there existed any legitimate barrier to reaching them. For Kristin, being blind was not synonymous with having an excuse.

---

108 Carmen Nobel, "The Power of Rituals in Life, Death, and Business," *Harvard Business School*, June 3, 2013.

She kept dreaming big and attended Harvard Law School in 2011. Through her education, how she fit into the law-making world as a disabled person started to have a profound meaning. It was in her law school classes that Kristin first became cognizant of how laws and policies were specifically affecting her life, for good and for bad.

Specifically, she learned about the legal concepts in torts and criminal law and how they applied to her own Labrador retriever guide dog, Zoe. Similar to the Robert Frost poem "Mowing," where the narrator's scythe is the instrument by which mowing is realized, Kristin's guide dog Zoe is legally a tool that is an extension of herself to accomplish her goals. But more so than legally, Zoe has served Kristin as an emotional and psychological support and again. Similar to the man's use of the scythe, the utilization of Zoe for Kristin in and of itself brings about purpose and meaning. In other words, Zoe fulfills the role of providing a supportive environment for Kristin to continue practicing her own strengths and abilities to their fullest, ultimately helping her to navigate the changes associated with this "new normal."

Zoe is an incredibly brilliant dog and has helped Kristin make countless complex decisions when navigating the world around her, whether stopping to avoid oncoming traffic, or even piloting Kristin back to a coffee shop in Geneva they had only been to once before over a year and a half ago. Zoe has been an instrumental part of Kristin's ability to continue expressing life fully. Of course, Zoe is a radically useful tool for Kristin, but just her supportive presence brings joy. In Kristin's words, "It's hard to be around (Zoe) without being happy, she's constantly wagging her tail. . . . she really allows me to be grounded and go back to mindfulness and presence and positivity no matter what we face. I can't even put it into words."

As Kristin continues to take part in the world around her, traveling to different countries or heading to a local restaurant, she doesn't have to go very far to face environments that aren't as supportive. She's experienced discrimination that is the result of a lack of education and understanding of those with disabilities. A simple trip to the grocery store, for example, or a visit to a website for online shopping, reveals the difficulty in accessibility for those with visual impairments. Several times Kristin has experienced Uber or Lyft drivers unwilling to accept her and Zoe into their vehicle.

Lack of accessibility for all has impacted Kristin's life at the personal level, but Kristin still believes in both a world that can be more democratized for all and her own ability to create such a world. She seeks to generate such an impact in her work today as a lawyer and disability advocate.

Like Delaney tackling the massive problem of global warming, the topic of accessibility is also an incredibly large-scale problem. The World Report on Disabilities reports that more than one billion people in the world live with some form of disability, of which two hundred million experience "considerable difficulty in functioning." Moreover, the report states:

"Across the world, people with disabilities have poorer health outcomes, lower education achievements, less economic participation and higher rates of poverty than people without disabilities. This is partly because people with disabilities

experience barriers in accessing services that many of us have long taken for granted, including health, education, employment, and transport as well as information. These difficulties are exacerbated in less advantaged communities. To achieve the long-lasting, vastly better development prospects that lie at the heart of the 2015 Millennium Development Goals and beyond, we must empower people living with disabilities and remove the barriers which prevent them participating in their communities; getting a quality education, finding decent work, and having their voices heard."

It's clear that lack of accessibility is a complex problem. However, one of the report's recommendations is to simply involve those with disabilities in the process of generating better outcomes.[109] That's precisely what Kristin is trying to do herself.

Kristin, and others with any kind of disability, are uniquely endowed to provide the world diverse insights about their disabilities and should be actively involved in formulating policies or laws around them. Having personally experienced the barriers of living with a disability and having the educational background to give her the ability to create change within the legal realm of policy-making, Kristin is actively executing her hope of creating a better world. She's passionately committed to tackling problems she's experienced personally, driving the advancement of human rights for all.

Kristin has taken an active role as an ambassador for those groups who have historically been and currently are disen-

---

109 "World Report on Disability," *World Health Organization*, 2011.

franchised, suppressed, or oppressed. Coming full circle from her weekend bike venture at summer camp, Kristin expresses this passion today in the bike racing community. She became plugged into the bike racing community and the supportive environment of those within it, who accepted her regardless of her impairment. The bicycle, like Zoe, serves as an extension of Kristin, continuing to empower her even through the loss of sight. Specifically, Kristin utilizes the tandem bicycle, where she puts all of her trust in a pilot who guides her at high speeds on the road or velodrome. In her own words, she emphasizes the power of the community, saying that, "The best part about being a blind athlete is that it makes cycling and most sports a team sport."

The cycling community, like Kristin's parents who signed her up for the weekend bike ride years before, believed in her and her ability to succeed, and again, provided a culture that allowed Kristin the freedom to utilize her talents to the fullest potential. Nonetheless, riding a bike at high speeds simply for pleasure isn't quite the end goal for her. That voice inside her that says she can achieve whatever she sets her mind on still propels her to accomplish her goals. She's competed in various national para-championship races, and currently, she's training to try out for the Paralympics.

As she continues to raise awareness for marginalized groups and help draft policy and design strategy to bring equity to all people, she will undoubtedly continue to lean on her own self-efficacy and sense of belief that she is capable of bringing about change not only in herself, but in the world at large. Somewhere inside all of us, we want to achieve something spectacular, and even amidst the personal change of vision loss, Kristin is doing just that. As she puts it, "No matter how different we are, our goals are very similar in the end, and that's what can bring us together."

***

One ancient Greek myth, as most notably written in Ovid's *Metamorphoses,* tells the story of Pygmalion, a legendary king and sculptor who created a female sculpture. Finding it both beautiful and realistic, he fell in love. On the day of the festival of Venus, who is the goddess of love, fertility, and prosperity, Pygmalion entered the alter of Aphrodite, where he made offerings and pleaded that he find a woman like his statue, with, "the living likeness of my ivory girl." Once home, he kissed the statue, and found that it lost its hardness and had come alive. Although rather illustrative and particularly unrealistic in nature, the root of this story is to display the concept of belief as expressed by the Greek values of loyalty and faith, on which Pygmalion's actions are based.

Yet, as mentioned before with the lyrics to the R. Kelly hit, "I Believe I Can Fly," it's not really as simple as *hoping* for something to happen, and then it somehow magically *does* happen. As we've seen from Delaney and Kristin's stories, the power lays in their ability to execute their own belief in the form of tangible action. In many cases beyond the stories of these inspiring women, believing can greatly affect external outcomes, catalyzing a change and helping us more effectively navigate environmental changes happening around us. For Pygmalion, this meant that his dream for his statue to become alive became a reality.

This story of Pygmalion and the underlying theme of belief are the grounds for which the psychological concept "Pygmalion Effect," which describes the effect that expectations from others has on our own performance, was birthed.[110]

The term was coined by Bob Rosenthal, a research psychologist who spent the majority of his career studying the concept of self-fulfilling prophecies. One of his most notable experiments came about when he secretly snuck into his lab one night and hung signs on the rat cages, labeling rats either smart or dumb. He then tasked some experimenters in his lab with being assigned either a very smart rat or a very dumb rat and were instructed to run their rat through a maze, recording how well it does. The smart rats did almost twice as well as the dumb rats, which shouldn't come as a surprise considering, well, they're smart.

However, Rosenthal had actually labeled the rats at random, and even after testing for coincidence, the "smart rats" were no smarter, and the "dumb rats" no dumber. How then, did simply labeling a rat as "smart" result in such a significantly better outcome? It sounds like a thing of pseudoscience, but upon further inquiry, Rosenthal discovered that the *expectations* that the researchers had in their head about how the rat would perform resulted in tiny behavioral changes that had significant implications. For example, those assigned to the "dumb" rats handled them noticeably rougher and with less regard than those researchers assigned the "smart" rats, who tended to be more gentle and caring to the little creature.[111]

110 Virginia Gorlinski, "Pygmalion," *Encyclopedia Britannica*.
111 Liana Simstrom, "WATCH: Can You Affect Another Person's Behavior with Your Thoughts?," *NPR*, September 7, 2018.

In other words, the researchers with the "smart" rats believed in their ability to succeed more than those researchers working with the "dumb" rats. Turns out, in the stories we've explored, it was the concept of belief, which includes the underlying strengths that the women exhibited and the environment under which those strengths were utilized, that made all the difference. As American inventor Charles Kettering puts it, "High achievement always takes place in the framework of high expectation."[112] As we've seen through *The Female Advantage* as expressed by Delaney and Kristin's experiences, there's a power in widening our beliefs about what we think we can accomplish because doing so can result in reaching an outcome we didn't initially believe we were capable of.

---

112 "High achievement always takes place in the framework of high expectation," *statusmind.com.*

CHAPTER 7

SHE'S GRATEFUL

The best way to find yourself is to lose yourself in the service of others.

-GANDHI

In 1997, a fascinating experiment exploring cognitive bias asked one thousand participants whether they thought certain famous figures would go to heaven. According to the respondents, then-president Bill Clinton received a 52 percent chance, Michael Jordan had a 65 percent chance, and Mother Teresa was awarded a 79 percent chance. Interestingly, the person that the respondents believed had *the highest likelihood* of making it to heaven, with an average of an 87 percent chance among respondents, was none other than . . . the respondent themselves.[113]

Nonetheless, receiving an 8 percent lower chance than the average respondent in terms of going to paradise, Mother

---

113 Francesca Gina and Maryam Kouchaki, "We behav. . .ot more badly than we remember," *The Conversation*, June 7, 2016.

Teresa is widely considered by many to be one of the greatest humanitarians to have ever lived. Within the realm of the concept of change, there's a lot we can learn from her and her commitment to serving the world. Mother Teresa's capacity in experiencing change throughout her life can be explored by her choice to practice gratitude and a focus on something bigger than just herself.

In her words, she proclaimed that, "The best way to show my gratitude is to accept everything, even my problems, with joy."[114] Gratitude is an effective vehicle for fostering openness and acceptance for the changes going on around us, whether they be good or bad, and whether we can control them or not. As we'll discover, Mother Teresa's expression of gratitude is what helped her significantly on her journey of helping others.

Many of us have been conditioned since birth to display the principles of gratefulness. As I recall, my childhood experience of opening up birthday gifts from family illuminates this sentiment. As I unwrapped my gifts, I can still hear my mom's voice perfectly clear:

"Now, what do we say?"

I looked down at the gift that I absolutely hated. I wanted the *other* coloring book. Luckily, I see a receipt taped on the back of the package, and my dimples begin to surface.

"Thank you!"

---

114 Philip Kosloski, "7 Saintly quotes about being thankful," *Aleteia*, November 19 2017.

The simple clichés of "being grateful," or "not taking anything for granted," or even "a little help goes a long way," all point us to humanity's inclination to express elements of goodness in society. For as simple as they are, and oftentimes as inauthentic as they can be, the underlying attitudes of being grateful and practicing gratitude by way of helping others has very tangible benefits. Even on the personal level, research has even found emotional benefits for us practicing gratitude and helping others.

We've all felt happiness or ecstasy when we are experiencing an intense wave of gratitude or happiness from doing something for others. Maybe it was a beautiful sunrise or paying for the coffee of the person behind you in line at Starbucks.

But when was the last time you explicitly wrote a letter of thanks to someone, or verbalized exactly *why* you are grateful to someone in your life? It appears that there's some kind of gap between the gratitude we feel within ourselves and the outward actions we make toward others to ensure they are aware of our gratefulness. In Mother Teresa's story, we'll see how the gap between our inherent gratitude and resulting actions can be bridged through the practice of serving others. I argue that for everyone, a pivot toward the practice of authentic displays of gratitude would benefit all.

As humans, we have a choice to express our feelings in the form of actions, or in this case, choosing to practice gratitude and finding ways to help others that leads us to our ability to cultivate more of both. This philosophy of "choosing" not only exists in our minds but can also be integrated into our daily lives.

For Mother Teresa, her philosophy on gratitude revolved around the centrality of her Catholic faith, which held the underlying value of focusing on what she could *give* rather than *what she was receiving.* She often talked about how grateful she was to serve the sick in the slums of Calcutta, India, because it enabled her to deepen her spirituality. This essence of "grateful giving" is best expressed in her own words:

"It is not how much we do,
but how much love we put in the doing.
It is not how much we give,
but how much love we put in the giving."[115]

In Mother Teresa's story, the principles of gratitude and helping others are inextricably intertwined. The spirit of gratitude that she had is what spurred her to develop a heart for providing for those with less than herself. Her focus on serving others also helped her cultivate more gratitude. Both values complement each other and simultaneously caused each to grow and develop to deeper levels.

Although much of Mother Teresa's documented life is teeming with the themes of giving with gratitude, her upbringing is largely undocumented. We know that she was born in 1910 and grew up in Skopje, the capital of the Republic of Macedonia, where she felt from a young age that she was being called to become a nun. Her father's sudden death when she was eight years old greatly influenced the rest of her upbringing, which was solely through her mother. Her mother's firm belief and involvement in her local church instilled in Mother

---

115   Jone Johnson Lewis, "Mother Teresa Quotes," *ThoughtCo*, June 14, 2017.

Teresa a commitment to serving others and affirmed her own involvement in her congregation.

At eighteen, she joined a group of nuns in Ireland called the Sisters of Loreto, officially became a nun, and then traveled to Calcutta, India, in 1929 to begin her role as a missionary and began teaching at St. Mary's School for Girls. While in India, she was exposed to large-scale poverty and harsh living conditions as well as prolific socio-economic and religious inequities.[116] The Bengal Famine and the Hindu/Muslim violence were both significant factors that spurred Mother Teresa to changing her vocation.

The Bengal Famine in 1943 introduced her to mass malnutrition, population displacement, and lack of proper health care. This famine resulted in an estimated 2.1–3 million deaths over the course of a year.[117] Mother Teresa's sisters surmised that, "It may have been the Great Famine in Bengal and its aftermath, or the distress of the poor children in St. Teresa's School and all around, that awoke in Mother Teresa the great desire to do for the poor even more than she was doing at St. Mary's."[118]

Additionally, the widespread Hindu/Muslim violence brought Mother Teresa toward a newfound focus on the poor and disenfranchised in Calcutta. In 1946, the Indian Independence Movement reached its height. On August 16, Muhammad

---

116 "Mother Teresa Biography," *Biography.com*, April 27, 2017.
117 Tirthankar Roy, "The Bengal Famine of 1943," *History Today Volume 69*, July 7, 2019.
118 "Bengal famine inspired love for the poor," *The Irish Times*, September 8, 1997.

Ali Jinnah, leader of the Muslim League, announced "Direct Action" day, stating, "We do not want war. If you want war, we accept your offer unhesitatingly. We will either have a divided India or a destroyed India." During this day, widespread riots broke out in Calcutta, where Mother Teresa resided at the time. Four thousand people lost their lives, and one hundred thousand residents were left homeless.[119]

In 1946 on her journey to an annual retreat, she experienced "a call within a call." Moved by the conditions of the poor and destitute, and stirred by her relationship with God, she was inspired to pivot from her years of teaching to serving "the unwanted, the unloved, the uncared for" in Calcutta. This change, which some could be described as large and negative and potentially *life-threatening* in nature, brought Mother Teresa into the slums for the first time, where she washed the sores of children, cared for people lying on the side of the road, and nursed the sick.

Nonetheless, even though this change seemed to have brought about significant hardship for Mother Teresa, as she navigated the difficult circumstances of the streets of Calcutta, she actively chose it for herself. Within this self-elected hardship, this change would end up having far-reaching positive benefits, as eventually, her former students took notice, and one by one, joined her in her servitude.

In 1952, she opened up her first home for the dying in Calcutta, which provided a means for people to pass away with

---

119 Rosheena Zehra, "Direct Action Day: When Massive Communal Riots Made Kolkata Bleed," *The Quint*, August, 24, 2016.

dignity and respect. Within the next forty-five years, four thousand nuns would join in the mission of the home, joining forces and opening orphanages, AIDs hospitals, and charity centers all around the world. Although Mother Teresa died in 1997, her widespread impact and grateful heart are still remembered today.[120]

Without Mother Teresa's practice of gratitude and dedication to serving others, which catalyzed her pivot toward serving the sick and destitute on the streets, her impact on the world today would surely not have been as extraordinary.

***

The word gratitude itself derives from the Latin word *gratia*, which means grace, graciousness, or gratefulness and is best exemplified by the phrase, "ex gratia," which means something that is done voluntarily, or "out of grace."[121] For Mother Teresa, she knew that even the simplest expressions of care *ex gratia* toward others is what one should strive for, even if it brings you into uncomfortable and even undesirable circumstances.

For us, regardless of age or socio-economic status, among a myriad of other mostly uncontrollable factors, we still have the power to choose to practice gratitude and express servitude. Of course, this doesn't have to mean quitting your job and moving to a struggling community. We don't have to look far to find ways to help, and we can express service to

120 Sougata Mukhopadhyay, "Kolkata and The Inevitability of Mother Teresa," *News 18 India*, September 4, 2016.

121 *Online Etymology Dictionary, s.v.* "Gratitude."

others right in our own local communities. For both Mother Teresa and you, gratitude can serve as the highest means by which people can care best for the world.

What's the benefit of practicing gratitude and how can I do so?

Other than the power of helping others and spearheading rapid social change to those in the world facing some of the most intense inequality and discrimination, there's a psychological case (as alluded to above) to practicing the discipline of gratitude and integrating it into your daily life. Some research points to gratitude helping to lessen the duration and frequency of episodes of depression, quicker recovery from mentally traumatic situations, or even stronger relationship-building.

Even simple acts of gratitude can go a long way. One specific study by a psychologist at the University of Pennsylvania had 411 participants complete various writing assignments, one of which was to write a thank you to someone in their childhood who had never properly been acknowledged. Upon writing the thank you, participants immediately saw a significant increase in happiness, which was greater than any of the other assignments, and the benefits lasted for a month. The study didn't account for the increase in happiness or well-being for those that received the letters, but it's not unreasonable to extend this logic to deduce it to be significant as well.

A financial case also appears to exist in the practice of cultivating gratitude at scale. Another experiment at the University of Pennsylvania divided university fundraisers into groups that either made calls to alumni in the same way it was always done, while the other group received a pep talk from the director of annual giving, who expressed her thanks and gratitude for the students' hard work. The next week, the employees who received the gratitude message made 50 percent more fund-raising calls than those who hadn't. This points to the idea that gratitude, beyond its personal benefits, is a factor in altering external outcomes at large.[122]

On the personal level, Robert Emmons, author of *Thanks!*, provides a general framework for cultivating gratitude:[123]

- Look for the good (Joy): Have a mindset toward positivity. Even if it's the simple things, think about what good exists in your life.
- Receive the good (Grace): Accept the good. When life seems almost "too good," it's easy to discount your "luck" and fall into a false belief that, "this must mean things are going to get bad really soon." Don't fall into the trap, fully accept the goodness you've realized.
- Give back the good (Love): Think of ways you can spread this positivity and gratitude toward others. If you feel grateful for someone in your life, express it. As one quote goes, "In the end, we only regret the chances we didn't take."

Within this structure, there are many tactical actions one can take to implement gratitude into your own life. You could

122 "Giving thanks can make you happier," *Harvard Health Publishing*.
123 Robert Emmons, "The Benefits of Gratitude," *Greater Good Magazine*, November 2010.

practice keeping a daily gratitude journal, writing a thank you letter, or meditating. Perhaps one of our greatest inhibitors to executing this framework is the concept of self-serving bias because it supposes when good things happen to you, it's because of something you yourself did, but when bad things happen, you blame external factors. With awareness of this, you can remember that gratitude is about finding the gratefulness you can experience internally regardless of external circumstances.

Today, many organizations promote the concept of gratitude in easily accessible ways for all. Gratefulness.org was founded with the vision to promote "a peaceful, thriving, and sustainable world—held as sacred by all." The organization hosts webinars, open-sources a library of resources, and even sustains a "gratitude lounge," with the front page titled, "Everyone belongs, and everyone is welcome."

Scrolling through hundreds of comments quickly reveals that the theme of this lounge is to uplift others, even amidst their struggles. Carla just had knee surgery a year ago and the doctor finally signed her off of treatment. Alicia responds with a note of congratulations and says, "Each day is a victory." Barb explains she's been struggling to find gratitude and asks for help. Mica suggests a book and includes the reminder that gratitude is a lifelong journey. Ose advises the group to "find strength to be and perceive yourself present with your natural gift of being who you are." And Diane responds with a heartfelt thank you.[124]

---

124 "Gratitude Lounge," *Gratefulness.org.*

Today you can ask Siri, Alexa, or another personal assistant for help ordering food, turning music on, or checking the weather. But those programs don't actually care or empathize with you, because they really are just computer-generated algorithms. However, a platform like Gratefulness.org completes the task of matching those people who genuinely care and are willing to give their time and energy in the form of encouragement or validation to those who are in need of it. These empaths find an authentic expression of care for others through this medium, and those seeking help receive it freely.

Of course, Mother Teresa didn't have Robert Emmon's framework in her pocket to utilize or the modern day internet discussion board of others seeking gratitude while she was serving on the streets of Calcutta, but she, and what seems like all gratitude cultivators alike, held a deeply imbedded belief system that served as the catalyst to nurturing their heart toward others. These people are aware enough of what was going on around them to capture the full expression of this disposition.

What it really comes down to is that gratitude, like all of the other principles we've explored, is a skill and ability that takes active effort in order to realize its benefits on your way to experiencing pivots and most effectively handling the environmental changes of life. Mother Teresa was a gratitude maximizer, and it required significant efforts from herself and awareness of what was going on around her in particular in order to actualize it. From her humble beginnings in Macedonia to becoming principal of St. Mary's School for Girls, to redirecting her life's mission to serving in the slums, she constantly went outside her comfort zone in order to question how she could be better for the sake of others, which maximized her ability pivot and serve others in the greatest possible capacity.

***

Regarding both the concepts of helping others and practicing gratitude, a "chicken or egg" debate could arise. Does gratitude facilitate helping others or vice versa? As we've seen, there exists a fascinating intersection between the proliferation of gratitude in one's life and analyzing how those same people tend to serve and commit to something bigger than themselves.

Perhaps even more so than understanding the actual relationship between these two concepts, what may be more constructive is to realign ourselves with the belief that there's a lot to be grateful for in the grand scheme of things. Most of us do, in fact, have higher GDP per capita and better health outcomes than our ancestors thousands of years ago, and even our grandparents a few decades ago.

Just being alive at this very moment required millions of years of advancement from the human species. Your ability to even read this very text implies a lot about yourself with regard to your privilege and your abilities. Even your very brain itself has astronomical capabilities and it's believed to hold over two hundred exabytes (One exabyte is equivalent to one billion gigabytes) of information, which is "roughly equal to the entire digital content of today's world." It's an almost inexplicable amount of information.[125]

But of course microscopically, it's in no way debatable that parts of our lives can be incredibly traumatic and depressing. But zooming out to the macroscopic, mulling over the miraculous nature of our existence and the human experience at large can create a change toward a mindset of gratitude and thus a change in our actions toward others.

Without a doubt, the state of the world today looks very different than seventy years ago, when Mother Teresa was doing the bulk of her ministry. However, the one thing that still exists are people and communities who need proper food, clean water, political stability, access to capital, or freedom to practice their religion, among a myriad of other problems awaiting solutions.

There's absolutely no shortage of people in the world who need help, and the human species is full of people with the intellectual, emotional, and financial means to help solve these problems. Whether it's simply your elderly neighbor struggling to walk to the mailbox on her icy driveway or your town struggling with systemic racism that goes mostly unchallenged, one does not have to look very far to find the inexhaustible number of opportunities needed to make a pivot toward being an agent for positive change.

---

125 Bill Bryson, "Why the most awe-inspiring wonder in the universe is inside your head," *Daily Mail*, September 7 2019.

Along the vein of helping others and our brains' capabilities to do so, it's worth mentioning the concept of altruism, which appears to be a biologically endowed characteristic in each and every one of us. The biological case of altruistic behavior has been an age-old quandary, going all the way back to eighteenth-century Swiss philosopher Jean-Jacques Rousseau who argued that we are "noble savages" whose goodness is corrupted by civilization and institutions. Seventeenth-century English philosopher Thomas Hobbes argued we are "selfish brutes," and only civilization can save us from our evil impulses.

The idea of altruism and the ability for humans to act with goodness without seeking anything in return has been questioned and debated for centuries. It can be argued that altruism isn't really altruism if the person acting altruistically has *any kind* of personal benefit such as something as simple as the feeling of happiness from making a baby laugh or a rush of ecstasy from jumping into a freezing pond to save a drowning puppy. But logically, do people really stop to question the personal utility they would gain when they selflessly enter a burning house to save a child? But that example, you might say, is one in a million.

How about when your coworker unknowingly drops some important documents on the way to a meeting down the hall, do you not instantly pick them up? (Well maybe not, if you don't like your coworker). It's valid to argue that in this example you pick up the papers in a response to a fear of punishment if you don't.

This postulation can be analyzed under various assumptions. Nonetheless, what's important here is that regardless of if we find ourselves personally benefitting from helping others or not should by no means stop us from doing so. It really all comes back to the idea of gratitude and understanding that when people act in kindness toward me, I am grateful and I project that same rationality when serving others.

One recent study at UCLA sought to explore the concept of altruism and found that our tendencies to engage in the practice of it may depend on the reactivity of certain parts of our brains to external information. The researchers scanned the brains of participants, particularly the amygdala, along with the somatosensory cortex and anterior insula, which are associated with experiencing emotion and with imitating others, as well as the prefrontal cortex, which is responsible for determining our behavior and controlling our impulses.

Participants engaged in the "Dictator Game," where each was responsible for allocating the resource of ten dollars to him or herself and a stranger for twenty-four rounds. What was found in the brain scans is that participants who were the most stingey, giving away only one to three dollars on average, had the most activity in the prefrontal cortex. However, the most generous participants, giving approximately $7.50 of on average, had the most activity in the part of the brain associated with emotion and imitating others. Leonardo Christov-Moore, a postdoctoral fellow and researcher on the project says, "The more we tend to vicariously experience the states of others, the more we appear to be inclined to treat them as we would ourselves."[126]

---

126 Meg Sullivan, "Your brain might be hard-wired for altruism," *UCLA Newsroom*, March 18, 2016.

Another study from the University of Washington recently looked at nineteen-month-olds and their ability (or inability) to practice altruism when provided with one of the most important biological needs: food. The test provided the babies with fruit and sought to observe whether or not they would engage in giving it up without being directly probed or prompted.

A control was established where the researcher threw a piece of fruit in the direction where the baby could pick it up. The researcher here did not display any expression or emotion. In this control, only 4 percent of the babies picked the fruit up and handed it back to the researcher. However, in the test group, the researcher threw the piece of fruit toward the baby, then made an exasperated effort to reach it, but failed. At this, more than half the babies tested picked up the fruit and handed it back to the researcher.

One more test was run in which the babies were brought in hungry, which would increase the tradeoff and "cost to self." Amazingly, 37 percent of those hungry babies still gave the fruit back to the researcher when they made a failed attempt to reach it themselves. It appears that even the youngest of humans and thus those the least nurtured by imprint-able human behaviors tend to implicitly express the principal of altruism. It's more nature in this case than nurture.[127]

Probably countless times you've "handed the fruit back," and acted altruistically without consciously thinking about it

---

127 "Altruistic babies? Infants are willing to give up food, help others," *ScienceDaily*, February 4, 2020.

at all. Fundamentally, that's altruism at its core. Time and time again we see humanity displaying heroic acts or even simple displays of kindness toward one another. Regardless of how one defines altruism in light of helping others, most everyone would agree that helping people feels *right*, or even more so, feels *good*. Eighteenth-century German philosopher Immanuel Kant puts it this way: "Many souls are so compassionately disposed that, without any further motive of vanity or self-interest, they find an inner pleasure in spreading joy around them.[128]

Even though, as seen by the research, there's probably an indeterminable amount of unconscious behaviors and actions we take part in that express altruism toward others throughout our lives, what shouldn't be disregarded is our own ability to pivot, like Mother Teresa did when she moved her vocation to the streets and choose to consciously serve others as an expression of our own gratitude.

***

Singer, rapper, and poet Raegan Sealy may be such a woman whose soul "so compassionately disposed," as Kant put it. In 2015, having never been to the United States before, she moved to New York City to study poetry. Living in the UK at the time, the only way to fund a master's degree in the United States happened to be through one of the most prestigious fellowship programs that exists: the Fulbright Scholarship. She submitted an application, continued to work and

---

128 Richard Kraut, *The Quality of Life: Aristotle Revised, Oxford University Press,* 2018.

perform, and eventually received the good news that she had been awarded the scholarship.

She imagined all of the things she thought New York would be like as seen in movies and other mediums, but once she got there, she quickly realized, "New York was dirty. And New York was expensive." After some more time, when the serious social issues of homelessness and the mental health crisis became obviously apparent to her, she questioned the reality of being conditioned to, "walk past people on the street that we should help." A lot of the time, she was left feeling discouraged. This newfound change in her environment, perhaps *Lego-esque* in nature, facilitated Raegan's realization of the unmet needs of those around her, providing her the basis to pivot and explore new ways to help her local community.

Further echoing the Immanuel Kant quote above, Raegan seems to be the exact type of person who greatly values helping others, and she found a way to use these observations to drive change for those who needed it most right in her local community of New York City.

While obtaining her master's degree, Raegan began working with those underrepresented and underserved groups in NYC, within schools and prisons, providing creative writing workshops so the participants could find their own voice.

Many times through her work she witnessed people open up with the things that weigh so heavily on their lives on a day-to-day basis simply through the act of putting pen to paper. A specific technique that has proven transformative in her experience was asking participants to write letters to both their past and future selves. The participants were able to inquire into their past experiences and hardships and open up in a safe space.

Raegan's experience isn't something only she has found the benefit in. The state of Louisiana leads the world, on a per capita basis, in imprisoning people. Zachary Lazar, novelist and English professor at Tulane University, says, "I met a lot of people in prison who were doing a lot of incredible, creative stuff. A lot of them arrive in prison with creativity in their background, and once they are there it is a release, a way to pass the time."

Writing changes the way the inmates feel, providing purpose and meaning, and opportunities for them to be defined by something connected to their creative abilities rather than the worst thing they've done. One participant describes the transformation this way, "Because of this experience in my life I was able to be reborn inside. And I am somebody that I never knew I could be now."[129]

For Raegan, she found the best environment for her to be reborn was in her community, through her work with empowering people to express themselves fully through artistic endeavors. The ability for humans to implement positive change right in the communities around them shows us that for as much negativity and hardship we see in the world or even experience personally, there exists people who genuinely want to help. In the case of the prison and education systems

---

129 *The Creative Brain*, 2019, Netflix.

in particular, Raegan has realized the power of creativity in the form of writing to help those in need, empowering them to find their voice.

Today, Raegan spends her time empowering others to realize their own potential, but there was a time where she was stuck in silence, struggling to find it herself. At thirteen years old, she began attending a music center for kids who weren't finding success in the conventional educational system. At the music center, a male teacher befriended her and appeared to care for her. What he was actually doing was grooming her and fifteen other girls. She describes the scenario in poetic detail in her TED Talk, administered in the form of a rap:

"He gave me money for my smokes and he listened. He really did. He picked me up from school and he bought me alcohol, and when he told me to take off my clothes I did. See, he used his words to herd us into a trap. Me and fifteen other girls kept abuse under wraps. But now I'm free, a bird and I use mine to clap back, get snaps, and empower other poets—that's what you are—through rap."[130]

This abuse didn't end until she was nineteen years old. She would enter a multi-year court case which wouldn't end until her last year in college. As she completed her final dissertation, she finally received the news of his prison sentence. In the midst of Raegan's traumatic childhood experience, she found a way to use her passion for others to empower them to find *their* inner poet.

---

130 Raegan Sealy, How rap saves lives, TED video.

For Raegan, she found her life's purpose through the arts, which have enabled her to find her own voice and open up about her childhood experience. In today's day and age, connectivity seems to be even more surface-level, given the widespread availability of a connection-at-your-fingertips world. Raegan is a pioneer in this space, unapologetically committed to helping others open up their deepest thoughts and feelings in the intimate and uncut way that writing, rap, and poetry allow.

***

Today, even though one need not look very far to find problems and issues in the world we live in, one also need not have to try too hard to bring solutions in the form of helping others in one way or another.

However, maybe you aren't someone who experienced "a call within a call" like Mother Teresa, or you aren't an extremely talented artist like Raegan. Maybe you feel incredibly discouraged by all of the destruction and problems around you and believe that you are imprisoned in your thoughts and frozen in your ability to act. Maybe, in one way or another, you feel *helpless* at being *helpful*.

A female management consultant we'll call Caroline was enrolled in a negotiation workshop run by renowned psychologist Adam Grant. Caroline is pinned a "giver," which Grant defines as those people who contribute to others without expecting anything in return. These people are true altruists. As good as it may seem, a main problem with being a giver is that you often put others' needs above your own, and Caroline in particular was realizing how this was negatively impacting her life. She wanted to ask her employer for a location change to New York City, but was fearful to initiate the negotiation at the expense of appearing to put her own self-interest above the company's.

A study by Harvard professor Hannah Riley Bowles illuminates Caroline's personal experience. After observing over two hundred executives in a role play salary negotiation, it was found that the men landed 3 percent more salary than the women, on average. The women were acting more like givers than the men.

However, another group of women were found to outperform the male group by 14 percent. *Why?* For this round of the experiment, these women were instructed to negotiate on behalf of someone they mentor. Being an agent for others propelled these women to a higher level of success themselves.

Caroline was successful because she was inspired by this technique. She mustered up the courage, and eventually successfully negotiated a transfer. She initiated the negotiation with the idea in mind that she wanted to move to New York City in order to be closer to family. It wasn't about her and her selfishness. It was about her family and the care she has for them.[131]

A simple change in mindset could be all we need to bring us to a new place or experience a radically different outcome.

---

131 Adam Grant, "In the Company of Givers and Takers," *Harvard Business Review*, April 2013.

In this case, thinking about *how* what we want connects to other people and our abilities to be helpful to those people gives us something inspiring to fight for. As Oprah puts it, "Helping others is the way we help ourselves."[132]

For all of us, it's crucial to remember the relationship between gratitude and servitude, and then seek out opportunities where we can cultivate both. We simultaneously function as both the *giver* of help and the *receiver* of help at different times in our lives and for various reasons. What lies within the space of these dichotomies is a change—either identifying someone's desires and needs and helping them, or identifying how others can help you meet your own needs and desires. As we've seen through *The Female Advantage* as exemplified by Mother Teresa and Raegan, there's incredible power in the act of practicing gratitude and helping others to be an agent for change, but the responsibility lies on each of us to use those abilities to not only bring about some kind of change, but to actualize the most effective changes possible.

---

132 "Helping others is the way we help ourselves. . .prah Winfrey," quotemaster.org.

CHAPTER 8

SHE DEFINES SUCCESS IN HER OWN WAY

———

Never discourage anyone who continually makes progress, no matter how slow.

-PLATO

How many times in life do you look around at others as a source of comparison and inspiration for your own success? It seems as though everything from work, to school, to social activities includes some kind of component of comparison with those around us. After a Harvard MBA and successful five years in management consulting, Sunny Stroeer realized it was time to realign her life around her true passions.

A word that arose from ancient Greek philosophers best describes the concept of her re-definition: eudaimonia. It explains the human state in which you're achieving your full potential. In one of ancient philosopher Aristotle's most well-renowned works, *Nicomachean Ethics*, he describes eudaimonia as "doing and living well."[133]

Today, as an extreme altitude adventurer and world record breaker, Sunny is currently living by this principle. However, it wasn't always that way. Earlier in her adulthood, in her career as a consultant, she experienced a project assignment that left her chronically burned out. At that point, she knew it was time to find a better way to experience her own version of eudaimonia.

However, Sunny's approach to finding meaning and purpose for her life is not necessarily a typical one. After working eighty hours or more between Monday and Friday for her job, and assumedly becoming mentally exhausted from pushing her intellectual capacity to its limits, she would spend her precious weekends pushing her physical capabilities.

She found her respite in the mountains, competing in ultra-marathon races of various distances, up to one-hundred miles, along with challenging herself further in other extreme outdoor activities like rock climbing and mountaineering. She realized her passion for these activities by pursuing her own definition of balance between her time at work and her time outside of it. By taking part in these epic ventures, she found an optimal way for her to clear up headspace that allowed her to be effective at her job again the following week.

133 Catherine Moore, "What is Eudaimonia? Aristotle and Eudaimonic Well-Being," *PostivePsychology.com*, November 2, 2020.

Maybe her extremist strategy toward her own version of relaxation isn't as crazy as it might sound. Her experience seems to align to the building evidence that participation in outdoor activities can help people concentrate better on daily professional tasks. Attention Restoration Theory (or ART for short), was originally proposed in the 1980s and 1990s, at a time when digital technology was beginning to connect humanity in a way like never before. Imagine leaving the physical office but not actually being able to disconnect because you are checking your email at home.

As the human experience has rapidly evolved over a few thousand years from spending a majority of time outdoors hunting and gathering or producing sustenance via agriculture, to now finding the best utilization of our time on laptops and in meetings, the interest in ART and the power of nature to heighten our human experience has gained traction.[134] For Sunny in particular, in alignment to ART, the experience of the outdoors and nature provided her a respite from her grueling job, which catalyzed an eventual change in occupations.

This yearning to pivot her career trajectory was further illuminated when the balance between her vigorous work environment, coupled with her pursuits outside of work, was compromised due to an exhausting project, which caused her to reflect on her own personal goals and vision for her life.

At the time, Sunny was managing a team where the project's deliverables and clients' expectations required

---

134 Courtney E. Ackerman, "What Is Kaplan's Attention Restoration Theory (ART)?" *PostivePsychology.com*, October 7, 2019.

one-hundred-hour work weeks. Finally, at the conclusion of the project, after the final presentation was successfully completed in the boardroom of the fiftieth floor of the client's office, everyone exited the room except Sunny. She strolled over to the windows and stared outside.

Approximately thirty years before this moment, three-year-old Sunny was doing the exact same thing. Staring outside the backyard of her parents' house in Obernburg, Germany, leaning onto the glass, she yelled, "I want to go! I want to go! I want to go!" It's hard to guess precisely where three-year-old Sunny wanted to be at that very moment, but that same burning desire to "get out and go" stayed with Sunny throughout her life and in the culmination of this moment in the client's office.

Staring out the windows, 700 feet from the ground, tears welled in her eyes as she reflected on the magnitude of what was just accomplished and the reality of how much it mentally and emotionally took out of her. She was acutely burned out, and in that moment, she decided to quit her lucrative and successful career.

During the following nine months, Sunny finished up projects, got her finances in order, and road-mapped what she would do after her last day. For Sunny, this new change would be largely positive in nature (*lottery-type*), but, oftentimes with any major life change, it wouldn't come without difficulty. The most significant thing she found herself having to overcome was the questioning and criticisms of those around her who she valued and respected. Her colleagues, friends, and even she kept analyzing the validity and logic of her decision-making process. Nonetheless, she kept her commitment, quitting her job with the goal of finding something that would bring her more joy and purpose.

Her plan began simply. She purchased a Chevy Astro van with the goal to travel on the road for six months or so until her money was exhausted. After that, she knew she'd have to reevaluate, knowing that there existed a high likelihood that she would have to transition back to the corporate American environment after her sabbatical. However, during those six months of travel though many of the United States' most scenic and diverse landscapes out West, she met Paul, her now husband, and eventually they both made their way to Colorado.

In January 2016, about a year later, Sunny launched her own business named Aurora Women's Expeditions (AWE), with the goal to bridge the gap between women and the mountains. The launch of her company was inspired in many ways by the lack of gender equality among the population of adventurers and mountaineers she observed. Specifically, Sunny recalls during her first solo experience, in 2014, summiting Aconcagua, the highest peak outside of Asia, she was met with many mountaineers along the way asking, "Where is your guide?" or "Are you here with your husband?"[135]

She recalls that she "was shocked how few women there were. The women who were around all seemed to either be with boyfriends or in guided parties—it didn't sit right with [me]. I decided then and there that I wanted to make

---

135 "Our Story," *AWExpedition.org.*

a difference." Sunny had experienced this discrepancy in the most intimate way: being on the mountains themselves. This seemingly small observation served as the crux of her company's mission, which provides expeditions specifically for women, empowering them to experience high altitude adventuring.

Sunny continually seeks to empower herself and push her own limits. Her solo summit of Aconcagua in 2014 wouldn't be the last time she'd travel to Argentina to face the daunting 22,841-foot peak. In January 2017, she set out from base camp and, just eight hours and forty-seven minutes later, ascended the 8,501 foot elevation gain to reach the summit, crushing the base-camp-to-summit female record by twenty-nine minutes.[136] Through her ability to pivot into new territory personally and professionally, and both literally and figuratively, Sunny was able to find a more effective way to seek out her deeply personal version of eudaimonia. At the root of her pivot was her ability to define success for herself, rather than by how others' might define it.

But that doesn't mean it's the end of Sunny's journey. For her, defining success is always an iteration of asking herself "What's next?" Records broken and barriers reconciled, she still aims for more. She believes that the only thing stopping her from accomplishing what she wants are the self-imposed limitations of the mind.

---

136 Seth Heller, "Sunny Stroeer Is the Fastest Woman You've Never Heard Of," *Outside*, February 1, 2017.

She concludes that, "One of the biggest and most empowering lessons that I've learned in my life is that when you talk about something and say, 'Oh, I wish I could do that,' there's two scenarios: Either you're just kind of saying it, but don't really mean it. Or, if you really, really, really wish you could go do something, for the vast majority of scenarios, stop wishing and start making your plans . . . start saying, 'I am going to do this.' Walt Disney echoes this idea, saying, 'The way to get started is to quit talking and begin doing.'"[137]

As we've seen from her story, Sunny was willing to actualize the large change necessary to find greater meaning in her life. Underlying her ability to pivot was the internally held notion of a definition of success she created for herself, even when her own version looked radically different than those of the people around her.

For Sunny personally, her next ambitious goal is traversing the South Pole. Not only that though, she also hopes to break the speed record for this treacherous journey, which is currently held by a Norwegian Olympic cross-country skier. There are plenty of reasons why this goal should be seemingly insurmountable for her, but that doesn't seem to discourage her. For Sunny, the sky (or perhaps, the southernmost point on planet Earth) is truly the limit.

***

What's holding me back from defining success for myself?

---

137 Kat Prokhorenko, "How to Quit Talking and Begin Doing.," *Medium. com*, December 20, 2017.

As we've seen from the compelling example of Sunny, one of the greatest barriers to being able to define success for ourselves is the fact that we are, at least in some capacity, bound to the restrictions of the beliefs and norms placed on us by our environments. Are we also bound genetically to this disposition?

The concept of nature vs. nurture has been hotly debated for years. English academic philosopher Simon Blackburn says, "When the hoary old question of nature vs. nurture comes around, sides form quickly."[138] Gabor Mate, a Hungarian-born physician, disqualifies the debate altogether saying, "In the real world there is no nature vs. nurture argument, only an infinitely complex and moment-by-moment interaction between genetic and environmental effects."[139]

Regardless of exactly how much of our orientation toward comparative behavior are caused from the environment or from the three billion base pairs of DNA code that exist in our 37.2 trillion cells, every human can find themselves naturally inclined to play the "comparison game," in one way or another, such as at your job, like Sunny experienced herself.[140] In the case of defining success for ourselves, it appears that living in a world that is inherently comparison-oriented could be a major inhibitor in our attempts at doing so.

---

138 Simon Blackburn, "Meet the Flintstones," *The New Republic,* November 25, 2002.

139 "Genes, Evolution, and Environment," *Vancouver Community College Learning Centre,* 2016.

140 Hannah Ashworth, "How long is your DNA?" *Science Focus.*

Social comparison theory provides a compelling framework to using this orientation toward comparison to our advantage. It explains that individuals determine their social and personal worth based off of those they perceive as being better or worse than themselves. You might compare yourself to others for many reasons, such as helping with your own self-development, motivation, or a positive self-image.

If some ratio of societal conditioning and our pre-programmed DNA are comparison-oriented, then perhaps it doesn't make sense to take action to completely destroy our tendencies to compare in an effort to define success in our own way. Because as much as we may try, we can't separate ourselves from our biological nature and it'd be of extreme difficultly to completely disentangle ourselves from societal values and norms.

Might we be able to change the way we think about comparison in an effort to make it more effective on our lives? For psychologists, comparison is divided into two sects: upward social comparison and downward social comparison. The first occurs when we compare ourselves with those we believe to be better than us. Upward comparison can be useful to improve one's current skill level at a task.[141]

You want to be the best basketball player in the world? Looking to eleven-time WNBA All-Star and four-time Olympic Gold Medalist Sue Bird might be a good place to start. You watch all of her games and highlight videos. You practice new skills and shooting drills each day, and eventually, you

---

141 "Social Comparison Theory," *Psychology Today*

see considerable improvement in your basketball-playing ability. Maybe you're not as naturally talented as Sue Bird, but by strategically using her as an inspirational source of comparison, you find newfound motivation to work hard to improve your skill level to a new level of excellence.

Downward social comparison, on the other hand, occurs when we compare ourselves to others who we perceive as worse off than ourselves. On your way to becoming the best basketball player in the world, maybe you look at those you've surpassed through the process to get to where you are now. When the game is on the line and the shot clock is expiring, you've already put in the work needed to maximize your team's chances of success. You ingeniously dribble through defenders and pull up at the three-point line. *Swish!*

Turns out, both upward and downward comparison are processes that have implications for how we define success on the individual level. One way or another, we've all been plagued by thoughts somewhere along the spectrum of, "I'm better than this person," or, "I'm worse off than that person."

In the upward social comparison realm, you can leverage the perceived success of a famous artist, a successful businesswoman, or even a friend to propel you forward on your own path to success. Being inspired by the efforts and outputs of those who have come before you can serve as the ultimate motivating medium.

You could use your awareness of downward social comparison to avoid undesired outcomes. Say, for example, you want to change your relationship with social media. Based off your awareness of research that links use of social media to mental health problems, you realize that you don't want to be like "those people," whose addiction hampers their mental health and emotional connections. In this case, you use downward social comparison to spur your change, unplugging your router for a few hours each day.

Clearly, the human propensity to be comparison driven is deeply imbedded in ourselves. Although it's both biological and environmental in nature, we all have the conscious choice to leverage this upward and downward orientation in a way that we see as optimal for our lives on a mission to define success for ourselves.

There's plenty of opportunity to begin being more aware of these patterns of comparison that rule our lives. As Eckhart Tolle puts it, "Awareness is the greatest agent for change."[142] Once aware, you can take tangible action, leaning into this tendency of comparison if you find it helping you or others. In doing so, you can begin to unravel your own intentions and goals for defining success as opposed to the ones that the pressures of society places on you with little opposition from yourself.

***

But how does one even begin to define something as convoluted as the concept of success? Ask one person what they define success to be, and they might mention values like

---

142 Marlene Chism, The Greatest Agent for Change, *Marlenechism.com,* January 22, 2015.

security and prosperity. Ask another, and they might explain their passion for animal rights and how their life is solely focused on this humanitarian ideal. Whoever you ask, you'll find yourself subjugated by an overwhelming heterogeneity of responses.

Florence Nightingale, nineteenth-century statistician and the founder of modern nursing says, "I attribute my success to this: I never gave or took an excuse."[143] Actress and author Julianne Moore reminds us of the personal nature of success, saying, "I think you feel successful when you're doing something well that you enjoy. And that can be anything." Oprah discounts the chase of success itself and tells us, "Don't be worried about being successful itself but work toward being significant and the success will naturally follow."[144] Maya Angelou believes success is based on congruence, explaining it as, "Liking yourself, liking what you do, and liking how you do it."[145]

Regardless of whether your own definition of success is similar to the above or if you're still working on your personalized definition, what's true is that the definition of success is dependent on the beholder of it. We've seen from Sunny's story that success is based off of finding deep meaning and fulfillment, and as we see with the quotes above, success appears to be radically different for everyone. We'll discover

143 Norbert Juma, "Florence Nightingale quotes on Life, Communication and Nursing," *everydaypower.com*, May 5, 2019.

144 Asad Meah, "50 Inspirational Oprah Winfrey Quotes on Success," *awakenthegreatnesswithin.com*.

145 Casey Cromwell, "How 7 Inspirational Women Define Success," *entitymag.com*, December 9, 2017.

below, in another powerful female example, that Natasha Nurse's approach to success is process-oriented. The power in a process-oriented view to success is that it allows us to iterate and change along the course to achieving some desired outcome. As Dwight D. Eisenhower puts it, in terms of this process-based approach to success, "Accomplishments will prove to be a journey, not a destination."[146]

Natasha is a woman whose philosophy on success is aligned to this ideal. This process-centered approach has helped her experience various iterations of success throughout her life and more effectively experience change along the way. Today, she is a successful entrepreneur, content creator, and coach at her company, Dressing Room 8, which is an online platform dedicated to helping women find empowerment through coaching services and online content.

However, throughout her childhood, Natasha faced many obstacles, beginning as early as age six with bullying. She recalls her hardship: "For me, growing up in the Lower East Side of Manhattan, I was one of the few kids of color in my school, so I stood out physically speaking, and I also started gaining weight at the age of six." As she continued through elementary school, her classmates would pick apart her clothing choices and her natural hair, which led her to feel like she never quite fit in.

Feeling like an outsider, she recalls it leading her to be a very studious and committed student, even though her classmates

---

146 "Accomplishments will prove to b. . .ourney, no. . .estination." *passiton.com.*

didn't quite place the same value on learning as herself. From this experience Natasha discovered her own internal will-power and ability to be comfortable in her own skin regard-less of what others' thought of her. At a young age, she began discovering her own version of success rather than one which was created in comparison to her peers.

Natasha's early success in the classroom was propagated by her parents' support for her. As opposed to *hoping* she would succeed, they *assumed* she would, and that there was essen-tially no other option. In fact, to nurture this belief, Nata-sha's father designed a fake newspaper with the headline "On September 5th, 1986: A Star Is Born," (there's some upward social comparison in action) that hung on her bedroom wall for the duration of her childhood.

Although the pressure of these large expectations may appear to be crushing, it seems to have been the launchpad to her future success and her definition of success at large.

For Natasha, she defines success as two-fold: First, did you achieve the goals that you set out for? And second, bench-marks. In other words, along the way of reaching that ultimate goal, did you hit many goals in the process? She defines these benchmarks as "teachable moments," which she explains as something that, "Changes you as a human being." She believes these teachable moments "put the grooves into your mind [and] into your soul." It's what makes you who you are.

Natasha believes life isn't some endpoint we must reach, but the accumulation of every moment we experience in between.

Success for her includes failing over and over again, but she's constantly seeking to reframe and change the way she views her mishaps and mistakes into those "teachable moments." If she's learning every day, Natasha says, "Then I'm winning." Put another way, in the words of motivational speaker Eric Thomas, "Fall in love with the process and the results will come,"[147] His philosophy hypothesizes that people are usually losing because they focus too much on the outcome and not the process itself on their journey toward success. Natasha understands that regardless of an end result, that most personal growth leading to transformation is often found in the daily iterations of mastering a task on the path of achieving the goal.

As we've seen from both Sunny and Natasha's story, what it really comes down to is that success shouldn't be an end destination, or something to be the central aim for achieving a goal. The embodiment of *The Female Advantage* for these women to effectively experience change is based on their abilities to develop a unique definition of success for themselves.

Whatever your definition of success is, it's valuable to see it as something that can be adaptable and changeable, just as you are. By defining success for yourself you can find the power to experience your own pivots in life. On the journey toward whatever you yourself deem as success, you must seek to iterate the idea of the success itself and not be afraid to potentially swivel to a new goals and new horizons.

---

147 Asad Meah, "50 Motivational Eric Thomas Quotes to Unleash Your Greatness," awakenthegreatnesswithin.com.

CHAPTER 9

SHE'S VULNERABLE

Whatever is fluid, soft, and yielding will overcome whatever is rigid and hard. This is another paradox: What is soft is strong.

-LAO TZU

Sarah Jameson once lived in fear of asking for help. During her senior year of high school, she went to the doctor for her yearly physical. As she stepped on the scale, she saw a number she never imagined herself reaching. She recalls leaving the doctor's office in shock, promising herself that she would never see a number so high ever again.

She shortly thereafter began the proven weight-loss method of cutting calories. However, she quickly became obsessed with watching the number on the scale go lower and lower, so much so that about every six months she would cut her calorie intake even more. Eventually, during her sophomore year of college, her mental state towards losing weight was transitioning into what would eventually become a diagnosed eating disorder.

Sarah was studying psychology at the time and, in her words, she "had an idea of how the brain worked and [that] things could happen like that, which made [her] realize that something wasn't right." One part of her brain knew what she was doing was wrong, and she became aware of the fact that she desperately needed help.

She mustered up the bravery to share her struggles with her parents. As simple as it sounds, her small act of courage to seek out help would be the first small positive, *lollipop-type* change that would ultimately initiate her lifelong process of healing.

After opening up to her parents, she began getting help from a psychiatrist and dietitian. After six months of treatment, Sarah believed she no longer needed assistance and was fully recovered. For the rest of her college career, she wasn't focused on counting her calories or exercising excessively. However, in 2015, when her then-boyfriend proposed and the stresses of wedding planning began, her dysfunctional patterns made a reappearance.

Then in 2017, she stepped on the scale once again and saw a number she never expected to see. But this time, it was on the *other* end of the spectrum. Again, the logical side of her brain spoke up, saying, *"Sarah, this is not healthy."* Once again, she knew she needed help and ended up reaching back out to her old psychiatrist in hopes of finding a recovery plan that would equip her with sustainable healing.

The process of rewiring her mind into healthy thought-patterns was a transformation of deconstructing those negative thought patterns that had plagued her every day, and she eventually learned to lean into the logical side of her mind, which recognized that how she was living wasn't sustainable or healthy. By being vulnerable and seeking help from others, she was ultimately able to realize the change required to bring her the healing she desired.

But for Sarah, her story doesn't end at seeking out the help she needed. Today, she uses her experience as the grounds on which she is able to help others. Through her growing blog *Starving to Strong* and social media base centered around wellness and healthy baking recipes, she's developed a following of tens of thousands of followers and viewers. Ultimately, her story serves as a platform of vulnerability catalyzing change, and inspiring others to be open to expressing their own thoughts and feelings in a more productive way.

Sarah's story is a singular example, though.

Is vulnerability always this useful to realizing change for ourselves and navigating the changes of our environments?

***

The ancient Romans would have a lot to say about this concept. The word "vulnerable" itself derives from the latin words, "*vulnerare*" and "*vulnus*," which literally mean "to wound" and "wound" respectively. The Romans wrote prevalently using this word in literature and poetic works as a way to describe war, pain, and death. No wonder the word itself makes me slightly uncomfortable. All of those things aren't very positive to ponder.

In 19 BC, Roman poet Virgil published *The Aeneid,* which comprises close to ten thousand lines written in dactylic hexameter. *The Aeneid* follows the story of Aeneas, a Trojan who throughout the story fulfills his destiny, becoming the mythological father of the Romans.[148]

In book four, Dido, the queen of Carthage and lover of Aeneas, is reduced to misery because she's been abandoned by him, while he's off in foreign lands fulfilling his hero's journey. In her despair, Dido begins constructing a funeral pyre and planning her suicide. She climbs upon the pyre, unsheathes the sword that Aeneas left behind, and throws herself upon the blade. Upon realizing what Dido had done, Anna, her sister, laments and says, "I should bathe your *'vulnera'* with water and catch with my lips whatever dying breath still hovers."[149]

Twenty-seven years later in 8 AD, Ovid, another Roman poet, published his magnum opus *Metamorphoses*, which chronicles the origins of the world. Book four describes the moment when the mortal hero Perseus slays the sea monster in a descriptively graphic battle scene:

"[Perseus] attacked the creature's back, and, as it roared, buried his sword, to the end of the curved blade, in the right side of its neck. 'Vulnere' by the deep wound, now it reared high in the air . . . Perseus evades the eager jaws on swift wings, and strikes with his curved sword wherever the monster is exposed . . . The

---

148 "The Aeneid, Book IV," sparknotes.com.

149 Virgil, "The Aeneid," *poetryintranslation.com*, 2002.

beast vomits seawater mixed with purplish blood . . . he drives his sword in three or four times, repeatedly."[150]

How can a word with Latin roots in ancient warfare, epic creation poetry, and drama literature be reduced to the mass-marketed feel-good concept it is in this day and age? Today, in what seems like a "vulnerability revolution," the definition still holds, as *Merriam-Webster* defines the word vulnerable as: "capable of being physically or emotionally wounded."[151] Psychologists, bloggers, and influencers alike are seemingly profiting on this word, with cliché quotes like, "What makes you vulnerable makes you beautiful."

As we've recognized with Sarah's story, vulnerability serves as a compelling principle to bringing about the changes in life we not only desire, but also need. Yet, as we've seen historically, vulnerability means you are susceptible to harm. That logic still holds true today. Jacquelyn Schneider, assistant professor in the Strategic and Operational Research Department and faculty member of the Cyber and Innovation Policy Institute at the Naval War College, takes the topic of vulnerability quite seriously, as her research within military strategy outlines how the information revolution provides nations not only a platform of military dominance, but also simultaneously a high amount of vulnerability for adversaries to exploit.[152]

---

150 Ovid, "The Metamorphoses," *poetryintranslation.com,* 2000.

151 Merriam-Webster online, s.v. "Vulnerable."

152 Jacquelyn Schneider, "The capability/vulnerability paradox and military revolutions: Implications for computing, cyber, and the onset of war," *Journal of Strategic Studies*, August 22, 2019.

And that's just one example. If you take a look at how companies devote entire departments and resources to managing vulnerabilities and potential risks, we can quickly surmise that the ability to protect systems, infrastructures, and entire organizations from vulnerabilities is of the utmost importance.

What can we learn from this view on vulnerability for ourselves individually?

The Centers for Disease Control and Prevention (CDC) has what they call a "Vulnerability Management Life Cycle," that outlines how to manage various digital security vulnerabilities. They describe an instance of vulnerability as requiring three elements: "A system weakness, an intruder's access to the weakness, and the intruder's ability to exploit the weakness using a tool or technique" (Keep this definition in mind, we'll be coming back to it soon).[153]

It's crucial to note that, from the individualized human point of view, it's significantly *less important* for us to take such extreme measures to protect ourselves. Yet, I surmise that it's not difficult for you to find your own examples of spending substantial amounts of effort to protect yourself from potentially psychologically vulnerable interactions.

Why is being vulnerable so uncomfortable? Brené Brown, whom you may recall from Chapter 2 regarding her research on empathy, is one of the foremost psychologists on the topic

---

153 "Vulnerability Management Life Cycle," *Centers for Disease Control and Prevention.*

of vulnerability. In fact, she's dedicated the majority of her career to this concept. From her research, she's identified several ways that humans avoid vulnerability.

She talks about the behavior she calls, *foreboding joy*, which arises when we experience something fulfilling and joyful, but suddenly become awakened to the fact that this can't last forever, and because something is going so well, it must mean that something is about to go wrong. As humans, we create a psychologically self-sabotaging protective barrier that stops us from experiencing the joy of a present moment because we are scared of a future that can't possibly be as enjoyable.

Similar to this barrier, she also describes the concept of *numbing*, which is when we attempt to distract ourselves from authentic human connection with something else, whether that be drugs, sex, or social media. It can often feel easier to escape into the space of psychological separation that these mediums can provide rather than diving deep into authentic relationships with others. Even though it might not be the path of least resistance, early twentieth-century minister Joseph F. Newton emphasizes the value of fully leaning into relationships when he said, "People are lonely because they build walls instead of bridges."[154]

Perfectionism is a major inhibitor to vulnerability, as Brown says, "Understanding the difference between healthy striving and perfectionism is critical to laying down the shield and picking up your life. Research shows that perfectionism

---

154 "People are lonely because they build walls instead of bridges.", *forbesquotes.com*

hampers success. In fact, it's often the path to depression, anxiety, addiction, and life paralysis." *Foreboding joy, numbing,* and *perfectionism* are all protective measures that humans use to avoid the terrifying concept of vulnerability.[155]

Now we know what inhibits us from experiencing vulnerability, but what actually constitutes the human expression of vulnerability? We explored what the ancient Romans had to say about it, but the concept has evolved over the past few thousand years. It's best summed up with a story that Brené Brown was told by a man after one of her speaking engagements:

After six months or so of dating, a couple met for a dinner, and the man courageously voiced his true feelings toward his girlfriend and said, "I love you." In a tragic turn of events, those three crucial words were met with a, "I think you're awesome," and then an additional stab when the girlfriend says, "I think we should date other people."

He was devastated that Brené Brown's values of vulnerability and living courageously had backfired on him so horribly. As he drove home, he couldn't help but slam his fists into his steering wheel yelling, "Fuck you, Brené Brown!" repeatedly.[156]

Unfortunately, for this man in particularly and what we've experienced personally, practicing vulnerability doesn't always lead to a perfect result. As Brown says herself, "Vulnerability is not winning or losing; it's having the courage

---

155 Thom Belote, "Facing Vulnerability," *questformeaning.org.*

156 "Brené Brown Inspired One Young Man to Say, "I Love You," *Oprah Winfrey Network,* September 22, 2013.

to show up and be seen when we have no control over the outcome."[157]

Exploring vulnerability even further, let's apply the CDC's definition of a system's vulnerability to ourselves. The first element of *a system weakness*, as applied to us human, aligns to the idea that practicing vulnerability means internalizing the belief that you have fundamental flaws. Whether that be physical ailments, mental struggles, or behavioral problems, one must realize that they are imperfect.

The next requirement, *an intruder's access to the weakness*, applies in the sense that, as being imperfect by nature, you have the opportunity to share your imperfections, or in other words, to practice being vulnerable. Imagine you are mourning the loss of your job. The "intruder" in this case would most likely be a trusted friend or advisor who genuinely cares about your well-being and is invested in helping you in whatever way you need in your moments of dismay.

Lastly, the component, *the intruder's ability to exploit the weakness using a tool or technique*, is probably the most formidable of the requirements, because it is based upon the assumption that, by giving someone access to your flaws, faults, and vices, you also give them the opportunity to potentially exploit this information in a way that hurts you. What if the person you disclosed your employment status to gossips about it to her friends? That's principally exploitation of vulnerability in action. It goes without

---

157 "Excerpt from Brené Brown's *Rising Strong*: The Physics of Vulnerability," *parade.com*, September 4, 2015.

saying that on the personal level, when practicing vulnerability, we want to avoid an intruder exploiting our weaknesses at all costs.

Both timing and boundaries can make a difference when practicing vulnerability. Perhaps the timing of the man in the previous example's declaration of his love wasn't necessarily poor, but the key thing here is that practicing vulnerability opens you up to a potential *vulnere,* or wound, and when practicing being vulnerable, you have to be prepared for those wounds to potentially make an appearance.

Yet, the cost of not being vulnerable could very well be greater than the feeling of being wounded. What if the man had waited six more months to admit his feelings? The pain he felt for his love not being reciprocated probably would have been much more severe. However, as Brené attests, sharing without boundaries is not vulnerability.[158] There's a balance to be had. Like Sarah who courageously sought help for herself, we must refuse to let fear be an excuse to keep us from being vulnerable.

***

As we've seen, although it can be a painful or even awkward concept to wrestle with, vulnerability isn't something to disdain or ignore. Vulnerability means you are human, and there are incredible benefits to practicing vulnerability

---

158 "Vulnerability vs. Over-sharing: Where to Draw the Line?" *becomingwhoyouare.net.*

like building intimacy, aiding innovation, and provoking compassion, among a multitude of other things.[159]

Michelle Chalfant is another woman who knows the power of this personally and in her work as a therapist and holistic life coach, but she didn't always internalize the power of vulnerability as a way to promote healing and deepen relationships. She began her life in Rochester, New York, growing up with a family of four consisting of her mom, dad, and a younger sister of six years.

Her father was Italian, so with the familial tendencies that Italians stereotypically display, most of her family activities growing up ended up involving her extended family, including her grandmother, uncles, and cousins on her father's side. Her father's identical twin brother ended up spending a lot of time with her family. He and Michelle's father would work together every day, and they, along with more extended family, would all live together in a lake house every summer. Michelle recalls the summers as being filled with daily activities consisting of a lot of drinking and many parties. It all appeared to sound like a big, fun family reunion that never stopped.

However, issues began to develop when her uncle's behavior, which included anger management issues and alcoholism, started to have a negative effect on Michelle and her immediate family. Her uncle's behavior consisted of outbursts, specifically rageful and rude comments to Michelle's mom.

---

159 "6 Powerful Benefits of Vulnerability and Shame—Yes, you read that right," *intentioninspired.com*.

One of Michelle's first memories of this dysfunction consisted of a night at the lake house when her uncle had said something mean to her mom that resulted in her running to the bedroom in tears. Michelle, probably only five or six at the time, remembers providing consolation, saying, "Mommy, don't cry, mommy I'm here for you." Her father struggled to stand up for Michelle's mom, which resulted in Michelle becoming codependent with her mother at a very young age, almost acting as a caregiver herself and feeling complete responsibility to stand up for herself, her mother, and her younger sister in the face of her abusive uncle.

All of this dysfunction contributed to Michelle's high school and college experience consisting of a lot of anxiety and depression. She found herself spiraling into habits of heavy drinking, smoking, and developing unhealthy relationships as a way to cope with her family dysfunction. She remembers having feelings of hatred toward herself, as well as battling negative self-talk on a day-to-day basis that kept her feeling as if her family's dysfunction somehow made her into damaged goods unworthy of help, assistance, or love.

From the outside looking in, Michelle appeared to be a typical kid who may have been making some poor decisions. But on the inside, she was really suffering, and no one knew until she was twenty-one years old. During her junior year of college, she went back home for a visit and found herself crying spontaneously for no reason. She remembers her mom asking her, "What's wrong with you?"

Unfortunately for Michelle, the stigma around mental health assistance and counseling wasn't nearly as democratized in

1989 in the United States as it is today, where it is now widely recognized that one in every four Americans has a mental illness of some kind.[160] As she puts it, "There was not a therapist on every corner, there was no internet, or a way to Google a local therapist. So it was sort of like we had to 'suffer in silence.'" She recalls her dad's side of the family echoing this sentiment, saying things like, "We don't air our dirty laundry to strangers."

Additionally, Michelle's family members weren't the only ones who held this belief. This problem stems systemically from widely held institutionalized attitudes in 1980s America, which was a time of increasing divorce rates, rising reports of violent crimes, as well as an overflow of people into the prison system. At this time, usage of drugs like cocaine and the prevalence of AIDS were garnering widespread attention. All of this led to a variety of changes in the counseling and therapy space, including developmental theorist Erik Erikson's adoption of Freud's psychosexual theory into a modified psychosocial theory. What's important here is that Erikson supposed that mastering certain attitudes, skills, and ideas at certain levels of development would lead to an individual's improved well-being and ability to contribute to society.[161]

However, in 1989, Erik Erikson's model, or even other holistic models of mental wellness for that matter, were not yet adopted or even well known. What this meant for Michelle was that her anxiety and depression at twenty-one years of

---

160 Jenev Caddell, "Understanding the Stigma Around Mental Illness," *verywellmind.com*, June 21, 2019.

161 Saul McLeod, "Erik Erikson's Stages of Psychosocial Development," *simplypsychology.org*, 2018.

age wasn't viewed by mental health professionals as something that was the result of years of dysfunction and the chronic perpetuation of false internalized beliefs.

Michelle found emotional awakening in episodes of inexorable crying sessions that happened over and over. One time, she recalls, the crying happened at a Macy's. Her mom asked her why she was crying, and Michelle didn't have an answer. But she knew she needed help. She desperately wanted someone to talk to. Like the first step in the CDC's definition of vulnerability, Michelle recognized her own internal weaknesses and her need for help.

She was able to visit a psychiatrist shortly thereafter, where she filled out a lengthy questionnaire about her current conditions and symptoms. The psychiatrist walked in after it had been graded and declared, "Yep, you're depressed, here's your Prozac. There you go." In that moment, Michelle mustered up the courage to say, "I really just want to talk about my problems, like, what I witnessed growing up." Michelle yearned to, as the CDC definition puts it, give someone access to her weaknesses. However, her attempts at seeking out the help she needed were not being met effectively by the health care workers at the time.

The psychiatrist advised her to go down to the mental health center in inner city Rochester. However, social anxiety kept her from making the trip, and for the next three days, the Prozac gave her splitting headaches. At that point, Michelle convinced herself that she would have to figure out the problems she was facing in a different way than through the local psychiatrist.

During this time, Michelle was undergoing her own enlightenment about the human brain by obtaining her undergraduate degree in psychology as well as beginning to devour books about spirituality and the mind and body's ability to self-heal. She also found herself beginning to test out alternative medicine techniques like meditation, which propagated her own journey of finding inner healing.

Slowly but surely, she was beginning to unravel the traumas of her past and develop her own knowledge about what exactly was going on within herself. Her movement toward deeply positive, *lottery-style* transformation began when she realized her weaknesses and vulnerabilities at the same time she realized her strength and power to change.

She would take what she personally experienced into her career path, where she was better equipped to help others in their own traumas and struggles. Today, not only as a therapist and holistic life coach but also an author, speaker, and podcaster, she summarizes the diverse array of work she does as aligning to "grounded spirituality and simple psychology."

Michelle's journey to transformational healing in herself inspired her to create her own method for others called the "Adult Chair Model," which is a framework based on the three "chairs," of an inner child, adolescent, and adult.

The "inner child" is developed between the ages of 0–7, which is a time when we absorb everything like a sponge. The problem during this stage is that we absorb ideas, beliefs, and values without discernment. During this time, the map for our future is formed, which determines for us what is safe, what is appropriate, how we get love, and how we fit into the world around us. If our role models and care takers were wounded, the wounding also gets passed down generationally. The inner child chair shapes our worldview as we develop. If we sit in the "child" chair, we find our true emotions, true needs, creativity, trust, and intimacy.

In adolescence, our ego begins to develop, and we find ourselves feeling alone in the world as individuals. A need to protect ourselves arises, and when seated in this chair, we may become codependent, anxious, depressed, perfectionistic, judgmental, and/or controlling. We develop masks that protect us from the world, which don't come off until we gain the conscious awareness that we are even wearing a mask and are ready to transform and change.

The "Adult Chair" represents the highest version of our selves. It is our most authentic self. Here we are present and live with facts and truth versus stories and assumptions that we find in the egoic "Adolescent Chair." Sitting in this chair, we are capable of setting boundaries with firm compassion. Here, we become connected to the emotions or our inner child and are able to witness the thoughts and beliefs of our "Adolescent Chair." Now, we are able to make new, empowered choices. This is the place that allows us to become truly connected to our emotional triggers and negative conditionings. Here, you can realize your ability to direct your path and become CEO of your life.

The power of the "Adult Chair Model" is that we can ask ourselves, "What chair am I sitting in right now?" This question wakes us up into consciousness. As Michelle describes it, the model pivots us into the energy of the present moment, where we become a witness to our triggers and emotions. When we make a conscious pivot into the "Adult Chair" throughout the day and in different moments of our lives, we perceive things, like the concept of vulnerability, in a more rational and effective way.

For Michelle, her transformation occurred when she recognized her vulnerabilities and found the courage to seek help, which facilitated her inner healing. Her own healing process spurred her to bring healing to others. She has been certified in countless traditional and holistic modalities over the last thirty years and has a very eclectic view of healing and transformation, all of which opens up people to their own limiting beliefs and subconscious thought patterns.

Michelle's journey has served as the inspiration for her business. She prides herself on helping people get "unstuck," develop self-love, and live authentically. Her own life experience has guided her to develop offerings that break down complex issues and make them simple to understand, offering tools for healing that one can apply immediately to realize the positive change available within themselves. Her deep awareness of her own vulnerabilities is what aids her today in her work with helping other people sit in their "Adult Chairs" and live healthy, whole, and peaceful lives.

***

With regard to *The Female Advantage,* both Sarah and Michelle's stories are centered on the idea that being vulnerable and finding help is what facilitated the pivot necessary to achieve their personal healing. Within their own healing, they developed platforms with which they could help others with their own transformations. In alignment to the CDC definition of vulnerability, a recognition of our own weakness is what helps us find the help we need.

One Harvard Business Review article titled "What Bosses Gain by Being Vulnerable" explores this concept of vulnerability in the workplace through the story of Archana Parchana Patchirajan, a founder of technology start-up Hubbl. She had to announce the largely negative, *life-threatening*-type change of the termination of all of her employees when her company had run out of funds. Yet, in the hot job market of Bangalore, surprisingly, her engineers refused to leave, accepting substantial pay cuts.

One of her engineers describes his reasoning for staying with Archana, even after Hubbl was financially exhausted as being, "She knows everyone in the office and has a personal relationship with each one of us." As the founder, Archana was radically transparent about the company's struggles and treated each employee like family, so when the gravity of the company's finances became apparent, employees rallied together instead of breaking apart. As a tight-knit group, they stood by each other in the financial struggle, remaining both emphatically helpful and hopeful.

This example effectively demonstrates how openness and transparency (vulnerability) in the workplace creates a safe and committed environment for employees. Incredibly, a few years after her announcement to terminate her team,

Hubbl had a remarkable turnaround and was sold for $14 million.[162]

Being vulnerable and asking for help is hard but can be instrumental in better experiencing change for ourselves. I imagine you can probably very easily think of several examples of times in your life when you didn't want to ask for help, but once you did, were pleasantly surprised with the willingness of those around you to provide assistance. It takes humility to show your weaknesses and admit you need help, but as we've seen in both Sarah and Michelle's stories and the Hubbl example, it really could have life altering implications.

Today, the awareness and acceptance of vulnerability seems to be making a positive disruption across social circles and institutions. Take "The Vulnerability Challenge," for example. It seeks to be a "movement that encourages people to open up and be vulnerable on social media." In a digital world where it's so easy to hide under the mask of perfection that its user base and algorithms curate, the Vulnerability Challenge is functioning in a ruthless environment.

Nonetheless, the challenge and the hashtag #thevulnerabilitychallenge have amassed posts from thousands of people who are opening up and leaning into personal struggles that would have else been hidden behind the curtain of the digital landscape. Through this challenge, people all across the world are accepting and embracing their wounds as a means to find empowerment in themselves.[163]

---

162 Emma Seppälä, "What Bosses Gain by Being Vulnerable," *Harvard Business Review*, December 11, 2014.

163 The Vulnerability Challenge, *thevulnerabilitychallenge.com*.

Thousands of years before the Vulnerability Challenge and the rise of the awareness of the benefits to practicing vulnerability, a *different* ancient Roman philosopher was using the word *"vulnere"* (wound) in his writing. Emperor Marcus Aurelius, last ruler of the Pax Romana, wrote *Meditations*, a compilation of his personal thoughts on the stoic philosophy, around 170 AD. He writes:

"Don't be ashamed to need help. Like a soldier storming a wall, you have a mission to accomplish. And if you've been 'vulnerati' and you need a comrade to pull you up? So what?"[164]

Unlike Virgil or Ovid, Aurelius' use of *vulnere* isn't describing the gravity of suicide or the anxiety of fighting sea monsters. Aurelius is arguing to dismiss the ego, or that voice inside that says, "You aren't worthy of help," and, "No one actually cares."

If you haven't experienced it yet, at some point in your life, you will come to a time where you "have a mission to accomplish," and find yourself in need of some serious help in order to attain the change you wish to achieve. At that point, you will have to find the courage within yourself to speak up about your struggles and to be vulnerable enough to recognize that you are not only in need of help, but that you are worthy of it. As Aurelius says himself, "So what?"

---

164 Marcus Aurelius, *Meditations* (New York: The Modern Library).

CHAPTER 10

TELOS: THE ULTIMATE PURPOSE

We shall not cease from exploration, and at the end of all our exploring will be to arrive at where we started and know the place for the first time

- T.S. ELIOT

In early 2020, a clock lost twenty seconds. Usually, a clock losing some time isn't a point of major concern. The most likely conclusion to be drawn would be that a mechanical or digitized malfunction has been afforded to it. If it's a real clock, like the kinds that hang on a wall in a classroom, maybe it's in need of new batteries. If it's a digital clock, perhaps the hardware is crashing, or possibly the software was hacked. However, this clock isn't a digitized one on your phone or the one hanging in the coffee shop you frequent. *This clock is different. It's called the Doomsday clock.*[165]

Over 120 years before this, in 1898, Marie Curie, if you recall was mentioned in Chapter 7, and her husband published their discovery of radium. That single discovery had incredibly far reaching implications. Close to forty years after that breakthrough, in 1939, an elite team of engineers and scientists were taking part in a critical research endeavor in the small town of Los Alamos, New Mexico, in response to the growing threat of Hitler's reported creation of nuclear weapons during World War II.[166]

Due to the growing pressures and threat of a global war, President Franklin D. Roosevelt instituted what became known as the Manhattan Project, a government unit that eventually grew to over one hundred thirty thousand people in over thirty laboratories, to focus solely on the research and development of atomic weapons.

In New Mexico, the Los Alamos Laboratory's work centered around the Manhattan Project's top-secret Project Y, the project in which the atomic bombs were to be built and tested. After undergoing years of research and rigorous testing, at 5:30 a.m. on July 16, 1945, the first atomic bomb was detonated. Tangibly, the nuclear age was born. Metaphorically, the clock began ticking.[167]

---

165 Ryan Morrison, "Doomsday clock moves the closest to midnight in its 73-year history," *dailymail.co.uk*, January 23, 2020.

166 "Manhattan Project," *history.com*, July 26, 2017.

167 "The Trinity Test," *history.com*, April 23, 2010.

Nobel Prize-winner Frederick Reines claims that during his time at Los Alamos, he "worked in the company of perhaps the greatest collection of scientific talent the world has ever known."[168] The same brilliant nuclear scientists and engineers who invented atomic weapons during the Manhattan Project were the same men and women who created this seemingly faulty clock.

However, the clock was never really broken.

Its origins stem from the post-World War II era, when, in 1947, some of the scientists and engineers from the Manhattan Project convened at the University of Chicago, voicing their concerns and misgivings about their work. They compiled their thoughts in a pamphlet called the "Bulletin of the Atomic Scientists," which would be evolved into a magazine that year.[169]

The magazine needed an inaugural cover that represented the urgency of the concerns that these scientists had regarding the rapid evolution of nuclear warfare and the pressure to responsibly navigate the nuclear age. Martyl Langsdorf, a wife of a nuclear physicist who helped create the atomic bomb, accepted the challenge. What was created was the Doomsday Clock: a simple yet compelling design depicting a clock seven minutes from reaching midnight. The clock serves as a symbol for the world's proximity to global catastrophe.[170]

---

168 *Neutrinos and Other Matters: Selected Works of Frederick Reines* (New Jersey: World Scientific Publishing Co), xv.

169 David Welna, "The End May Be Nearer: Doomsday Clock Moves Within 100 Seconds of Midnight," *npr.org*, January 23, 2020.

170 William Yardly, "Martyl Langsdorf, Doomsday Clock Designer, Dies at 96," *nytimes.com*, April 10, 2013.

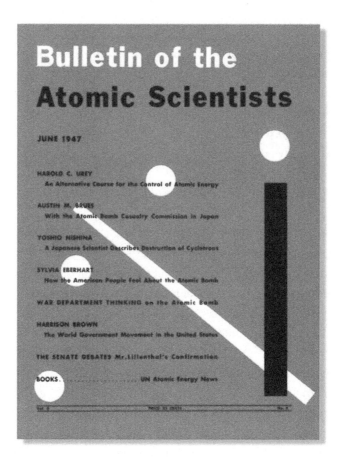

Today, this clock serves as the symbolic depiction of humanity's impending doom from threats both to humanity itself and our planet at large. Each year since its inception, a panel consisting of board members of the Bulletin of Atomic Scientists and a Board of Sponsors consisting of thirteen Nobel Laureates are taxed with making the crucial decision of whether or not to move the hand closer to 12:00 a.m. Today, the clock serves as the "universally recognized indicator of the world's vulnerability to catastrophe from nuclear weapons, climate change, and disruptive technologies in other domains."

As of the time of my writing, this clock is now one hundred seconds away from midnight. The Bulletin reports many reasons for the recent cut of twenty seconds. The main existential threats remain nuclear war and climate change, both of which have recently proliferated due to the "threat multiplier" of rapid technology disruption and eroding political infrastructures.

In the Bulletin's words, "We move the Clock toward midnight because the means by which political leaders had previously managed these potentially civilization-ending dangers are themselves being dismantled or undermined, without a realistic effort to replace them with new or better management regimes."[171]

Whether you like the idea of it or not, earth is not immortal, and neither are you. The clock is ticking, meaning, both you and your planet are approaching an inevitable "t=0."

What power do you have to change these things?

***

Around the same time that World War II was ending, Welsh survivor Dylan Thomas, along with his wife and daughter, found themselves in poverty and in desperate need of an income to survive. It was during this time that Thomas, a

---

171   "Closer than ever: It is 100 seconds to midnight," *thebulletin.org.*

poet, began writing and broadcasting his work on BBC radio, which brought him the income he needed as well as some fame.[172]

Under these circumstances, while on a trip to Florence visiting family, Thomas constructed his most famous work and one of the most well-known pieces of poetry from the twentieth century. "Do Not Go Gentle Into That Good Night" covers a multitude of ubiquitous themes such as life, death, and time. It most notably describes the inescapable human reality of death paralleled to the conscious ability to valiantly fight for life in the midst of those moments of dying. If you read his poem, you'll find that it teaches about the human power of practicing responsibility when faced with external changes that are, as depicted in the theme of death, mostly uncontrollable.

The application of Thomas' poem to today's present reality could be exhaustive. We don't have to necessarily face death ourselves to be haunted by the universal themes of dying or the fear of living with regrets. What's specifically provoking about Thomas' words under the basis of change and transformation is the "fight" that he argues for throughout. For you, it provides an opportunity to ask yourself, "How might I apply this mentality into my life?" and "What is truly worth fighting for or against?" The idea Thomas presents here is applicable to each of us today because it surmises that we all have a conscious say in how we live our lives and what we choose to be worthy of our efforts.

---

172 "Dylan Thomas," *poets.org.*

Nonetheless, as Thomas argues that death should be fought against, it's not the case in life that everything that *can be* fought against, *should be* fought against. The notion of effectiveness would be useful in determining what is worth fighting against.

A metaphor accurately sums up the idea. Workers are working diligently to complete the job of cutting through a jungle when suddenly the leader decides to climb a tree to take a look at what's around. Once having a full view of the jungle and the surrounding landscape, the leader horrifyingly realizes that workers are in the *completely wrong jungle*. Luckily, the leader has the humility to tell the team that although their work was right and valued, they were functioning in the absolutely wrong area. Essentially, they were being wholly *efficient*, but by no means, *effective*.

What this means for us is that we have a choice between what we deem worthy of fighting for, and simultaneously, a responsibility to ensure that what we are fighting for is an effective use of our finite time and energy. If it's not effective, that's when, as the metaphor goes, a pivot or a change in *where we apply* our efforts is required. A different environment, or jungle, is needed. I wonder if the engineers and scientists working on the Manhattan Project questioned the validity of the jungle they were functioning within at the time. The creation of the Doomsday Clock seems to point to the answer being, "yes."

Are you in the right jungle?

***

In 1940, seven years before Thomas wrote his magnum opus, then eight-year-old Walter Mischele found himself fleeing to the United States after the Nazi occupation of Vienna, the city he and his family originated from. He was living a seemingly *effective* life, graduating as valedictorian of his high school class and attaining an undergraduate and master's degree in psychology from New York University, as well as a PhD from Ohio State University in 1956. However, his education left him increasingly frustrated by the orthodox research methods of the time, which he believed failed to take environmental context into account.[173]

Does the environment in which we function really matter that much?

In 1960, Mischele took his talents to a new jungle: the test subjects of Stanford University's Bing Nursery School. With marshmallows in hand and preschool-aged children to utilize, the Marshmallow Test was born.

The Marshmallow Test is one of the best-known social experiments thought to have been created to display humans' impulsive nature and the economics of present bias, or one's tendency to choose a lesser thing now rather than a greater thing in the future. However, at the inception of the Marshmallow Test, Mischele had no such agenda to explain this fundamental human flaw.

The basis of the experiment is this: Place a marshmallow in front of a child, then leave the room. If they don't eat

---

173 Jeannette L. Nolen, "Walter Mischel," *britannica.com.*

the marshmallow, when you come back, the child will be awarded another marshmallow. From this simple test of will-power, correlations were found between those children who could wait for the second marshmallow, thus refusing the temptation of instant gratification, and their future outcomes of success in careers, relationships, and finances. Perhaps the marshmallow test can be a real-world crystal ball.

The result of the reports pointed researchers to the idea that humans are bound by ungovernable personality traits that determine their future outcomes. However, as we've seen expressed through the many stories of women and their own power to pivot and effectively experience environmental changes under a variety of circumstances, this isn't a valid conclusion. In other words, the test failed to recognize the *ability to change, grow, and develop.*

Mischele himself fervently denounced this widespread belief that the researchers held, saying, "That iconic story is upside down wrong . . . that your future is in a marsh-mallow, because it isn't." He explains that the point of the original marshmallow experiment was to show *how flexible*, and *not fixed*, humans can be by reframing the situation around them when making decisions. A simple change in the way the participants viewed the experiment resulted in substantial changes in the outcomes.

Mischele provides an example in which, during an experi-ment, a young girl couldn't wait more than thirty seconds before eating the cookies in front of her. But in another test, the young girl was instructed by Mischele that if she *believes* that the cookies aren't actually there, she would be able to better resist. Now, that same child could wait fifteen minutes.

There's something compelling about a shift in mindset.

For Mischele, his life and research has been about "showing the potential for human beings to not be the victims of their biographies . . . and to show in great detail, the many ways in which people can change what they become and how they think."

His research exquisitely displays the human ability to utilize our own power to adapt and change ourselves from the inside out by changing the way we view things from the outside in. As American philosopher William James puts it, "Thoughts become perception, perception becomes reality. Alter your thoughts, alter your reality."[174] It's easy to apply this logic in the comfort of my own Americanized upbringing, but is it possible to apply it to terribly inhumane circumstances?

Can a change in thought really make all the difference?

During the turbulence of World War II, which had brought about new innovations and ideas in both research and psychology, Austrian neurologist and psychiatrist Victor Frankl had his own opportunity to test his theory in a Nazi concentration camp.

---

174 Julie Carli, "Remembrance for Walter Mischel, Psychologist Who Devised the Marshmallow Test," *npr.org,* September 21, 2018.

Unlike Thomas, whose country of origin aligned him with the allied side, or Mischele, who escaped Nazi occupation in Vienna, Frankl found himself arrested and placed in a concentration camp in what is now the Czech Republic.

Before he was deported to the Theresienstadt concentration camp in 1942, Frankl grew up an educated man, earning both his MD and PhD from the University of Vienna, where he studied psychiatry and neurology. His research focused on suicide and depression, where he found much success in counseling high school students to virtually eliminate suicide.

Within the three years he was held prisoner at four different concentration camps, including Auschwitz, Frankl witnessed his research focus of depression and suicide on a more personal level than ever before. During this time, he was able to apply the same practices he used on high schoolers to prevent suicide attempts in the concentration camps.

Frankl was able to help inmates facing depression and suicidal thoughts by encouraging them to reflect on positive memories and joyful feelings. Astoundingly, the ability of those undergoing horrific atrocities in the camps, of which they had essentially zero control over, to change their thoughts, had notably positive results.[175]

Frankl's theory of logotherapy surmised that humans are centrally motivated by what's known as a "will to meaning" which relates to one's need to find meaning in life. From his

---

175 "Viktor Frankl (1905-1997)," *goodtherapy.org.*

personal experience, his research reports that even in the worst of circumstances, humans can still find and cultivate meaning. As he believes, "Everything can be taken from a man (or woman) but one thing: the last of the human freedoms—to choose one's attitude in any given set of circumstances."[176] Frankl spoke ardently of his belief that "between stimulus and response there is a space. In that space is our power to choose our response. In our response lies our growth and our freedom."[177]

Although it's not necessary for one to go through a traumatic experience to realize one's ability to be proactive in response to a change in their environment, as we've seen from all the stories of the women we've learned about so far, what's compelling in this case is that even in the most abominable of circumstances, freedom of thought and *the power to pivot* still prevail.

How can we practice this ability that exists within all of us?

We've learned that changes can be small or large, or positive or negative, and a function of an innumerable amount of circumstances both internal and external with respect to our lives. Practicing proactivity in the face of change has highly personalized meaning for each of us. It most certainly depends on one's background, upbringing, strengths, and weaknesses. Frankl's theory includes several disciplines to

---

176 Viral Mehta, "The Last of the Human Freedoms," *huffpost.com*, January 3, 2013.

177 Leslie Becker-Phelps, "Don't Just React: Choose Your Response," *psychologytoday.com*, July 23, 2013.

practice to aid in the process of realizing or reaffirming the freedom of thought that exists within you.

He mentions the concept of *dereflection*, which refers to the act of focusing on others in order to disconnect from self-absorbed thoughts. An example here might be thinking of the "big picture" when achieving a goal. Instead of thinking about how the goal will help you individually, might it be more effective to reframe the achievement by how it could help others or aid in some way to the greater meaning and principle in which you align your actions to? As you learned in Chapter 7, an external focus on others can bring about greater feelings of satisfaction and overall well-being in ourselves. It really is a win-win.

He also bases his theory on the concept of *paradoxical intention*, which is the fascinating psychological notion of bringing to mind the thing that one fears most and using humor or sarcasm to rationalize and objectify the fear. Growing up, I remember my mom often saying something like, "Ninety-nine percent of the things you worry about don't actually end up happening." I can't say with certainty if it's really 99 percent or not, but by reminding myself of this quote when my mind becomes entangled with illogical fear, a sense of relief envelops me.

Lastly, a key pillar to Frankl's theory is Socratic dialogue, which in this case is using the potency of words to lead ourselves to self-discovery.[178] As one quote goes, "Our

178 Arlin Cuncic, "An Overview of Viktor Frankl's Logotherapy," verywellmind.com, October 6, 2019.

words have power. They impact others, but they also impact us."[179] Through Socratic dialogue, one's preconceived beliefs are recognized via the words and stories they share. The stories and scripts that both those around you and you yourself create in your mind can be either crippling or inspiring (or anywhere in between). As goes this short illustration below, the interpretation and thoughtful analysis of words can have a lasting impact on our actions and outcomes:

A group of frogs was traveling through the woods, and two of them fell into a deep pit. All the other frogs gathered around the pit.

When they saw how deep the pit was, they told the two frogs that they were as good as dead.

The two frogs ignored the comments and tried to jump up out of the pit with all of their might. The other frogs kept telling them to stop, that they were as good as dead.

Finally, one of the frogs took heed to what the other frogs were saying and gave up.

He fell down and died.

The other frog continued to jump as hard as he could. Once again, the crowd of frogs yelled at him to stop the pain and just die.

---

179 Michael Hyatt, "Ho. . .mall Shift in Your Vocabulary Can Instantly Change Your Attitude," *michaelhyatt.com.*

He jumped even harder and finally made it out.

You see, this frog was deaf, unable to hear the others' pleas. He thought they had been encouraging him the entire time.[180]

Let's face it, we all have countless examples of how words and thoughts, whether coming from within us or from those around us, have greatly affected us either positively or negatively. Applying the principles of *dereflection, paradoxical intention,* and *Socratic dialogue* can help you not only recognize new ways to view the "space" that exists between external stimulus and reaction, but also lead you to arrive at a new jungle where you experience new and more effective thoughts about the change going on around you in relation to the changes you're experiencing within yourself.

***

As we've discovered through this book, the amazing thing about change is that it doesn't always have to have external manifestations in the form of radical behavioral changes or physical metamorphosis. Through the empowering stories you've read, I hope you are able to realize *The Female Advantage* in all of its magnificence. Women have an incredible ability to change, from the ways they've chosen to utilize the various principles and adopted the specific values that were outlined in each chapter. From what we've learned, I hope you realize how these principles can apply specifically to you and your life right now.

---

180 "Power of Words," *fropky.com.*

Whether it be from Martha in Chapter 1, practicing resilience as she navigated the death of two children; or Polina, in Chapter 4, making her way to the United States as an immigrant from Bulgaria and questioning the norms of society; or, Sunny, in Chapter 8, realizing how to define success for herself; I hope these stories serve as an inspiration to you and help you realize your own ability to change and navigate environmental changes in new and more effective ways.

For as much of the concept of change that we've dug into throughout these stories, I want to reassure you that change in thought is a powerful form of transfiguration. Perhaps the lack of awareness to this type of change is due to its nature of not being the readily witnessed or easily publicized kind. You may find these kinds of changes hard to recognize in others, and even in yourself. This is especially relevant considering society today, where we are bombarded with a plethora of advertisements, announcements, and content on a constant basis. Even a more recently coined term, "Dataism," reflects this sentiment with the conviction that everything should be measured and connected into a sort of "Internet of All Things." With all the emphasis on our smartphones collecting and measuring changes in our location or our smart watches analyzing changes in our heartrates, it's easy to believe that real change cannot exist or even flourish if you or the people around you *don't know about it* or *can't measure it.*

That's not true.

Perhaps you find yourself with the motivation to make a huge life change right now. That's great. Find a job that better suits your passions. End that toxic relationship. Move to a new city. Those are unrefutably some major life pivots. However, the simple task of learning and discovering more about the topic of change itself is a *change within itself.*

So congratulations, you've changed!

To dig a little deeper, what might be a fascinating idea to explore would be to undo your desires to quantify change as a means for your own self-satisfaction and feeling of accomplishment. Just think how many of the thoughts you have on a daily basis involve comparison to some other event or object: Is *this* food better than *that* food? Is *this* test score higher *than* the previous? Is *my* joke funnier than *my friends*? It's human nature to want to measure change, but I hope you can reflect on the idea that many changes are extremely difficult to quantifiably measure.

But that doesn't mean change didn't happen or doesn't exist.

Of course, this doesn't mean that attempts shouldn't be made to measure these types of invisible and internalized changes. It just seems to be a more complicated process at this time in history. Perhaps one day in the future, we will be able to download our thought patterns into a nice and pretty online dashboard to track our intellectual or emotional improvements over time, but for now, we don't really know how to measure psychological shifts in thought patterns like kindness or altruism. For sifting through the topic of change, whether it can be perfectly measurable or not, I echo twentieth-century British writer and speaker Alan Watts when he says, "The only way to make sense of change is to plunge into it, move with it, and join the dance."[181]

What this means for all of us who accept this as truth, is that we are bound to the responsibility and duty to lean in to change and join the dance ourselves. If change is inevitable, then we might do ourselves a favor by embracing it.

Yes, some changes are physical in nature like Gitanjali's iterations on her lead detection device in Chapter 3, or Kristin's progression into blindness in Chapter 6, but if you look beyond the physical act of witnessing something external, you arrive at something that is harder to notice and increasingly abstract in nature: the experience of an inward transformation. Within these tangible external changes that we experience are less observable internal changes for all of us. Think of it this way: If I break my leg in a car accident, won't my mind change too? Or, in a more positive lens, if I win the lottery, won't my mind change as well?

Those internal changes are just as powerful, and perhaps even more meaningful, than the external changes we face throughout our lives.

It's in this inward-facing analysis of change, although as mentioned, not perfectly quantifiable, that you can uncover and attempt to see yourself as you are, in order to help figure out who you might want to be, and how you might want to evolve.

---

181 Jackie Haywood, "The Dance of Change," *illuminateyou.co.uk*, August 30, 2019.

Telos, as is the chapter's namesake, is a Greek word that means "end," but also translates to "goal" or "purpose." We're arriving at the *telos*. At this point, I could recount all of the themes of pivoting that women express and that I have shared with you throughout this journey. I could make an impassioned effort to remind you how absolutely groundbreaking practicing the principles we've discovered are to your own ability to change. I could wrap up this journey with a nice summary of where we've been and where you might be going.

I'm not going to do such things.

I think it would be rather ineffective and a disservice to you as a reader. Doing so would undermine the overarching thread I've been pointing to throughout this book as expressed through the stories I've shared. Simply put, here's my *telos*:

You yourself already hold the power to pivot.

Ironically, you don't have to make a major change to choose to practice this ability for yourself. You don't have to wait until the "perfect moment" to be innovative or encounter a major life crisis to embrace vulnerability. I wholeheartedly believe that nothing is *really* stopping you from practicing any of these principles right this very moment. But, although none of the principles I've shared with you are too challenging to grasp from a theoretical standpoint, in practice, they are rather challenging to master.

From what you've read and learned, I hope you realize that real, sustainable change for yourself doesn't need to be something that is reduced to a valiant emotional appeal that leaves your heart racing with excitement and newfound motivation to go out and change the world. The scope of change I've sought to awaken you to throughout this book is a subtle, thoughtful, and calculated kind. It takes time and patience.

It's not a "post-on-social-media-about-your-New-Year's-resolution" kind of change, it's a type of change that is assimilated into your entire being. It's based on logic and reason and can only be had through the creation of new thought patterns that manifest themselves as actions.

And these actions aren't the final "check box" for your goal to run that marathon or get that dream job. The themes and principles of transformation you've explored, although not necessarily perfectly measurable in and of themselves, are all ideals that, I believe, and as Dylan Thomas puts in his poem, both *can* and *should* be "raged" for.

***

Over two thousand five hundred years ago, Greek philosopher Heraclitus wrote the well-known proverb, "Change is the only constant."[182] With the Doomsday Clock inching closer and closer to the inexorable truth of the end, I challenge you to seek out new beginnings. Whether small or large, or negative or positive, change is inevitable.

So what kind of change do you want to create?

---

182 Joshua J. Mark, "Heraclitus of Ephesus," *ancient.eu*, July 14, 2010.

This will most certainly require you to ask some rather important questions like "Who am I?" or "What is my purpose?" You will have to look at yourself and your life objectively, which can be a challenging endeavor, but, I believe, a supremely worthwhile one.

Let's be honest. The principles of change you've read about aren't necessarily earth-shattering in nature. But what can, without a doubt, be revolutionary in nature, is *you*. The principles in and of themselves hold no power without someone who can responsibly act on them and yield good by utilizing them. You are your own toiler of these principles, and both you, and the world at large, the harvester of the fruits that come from them. The clock is ticking. What are you waiting for?

ACKNOWLEDGMENTS

This book was an enormous undertaking. Without the support of so many people, it wouldn't exist. I have innumerable thanks to give but will only name a fraction of those people here. It goes without saying that if you (yes, you!) have played any kind of role in my life whatsoever, it has shaped me in some way as an individual, and thus, has shaped my book. I am incredibly grateful to have you in my life.

I first and foremost give my highest thanks to God as my creator, protector, redeemer, and savior. I believe He has blessed me greatly, and with that, I live with the utmost responsibility to share His blessings with others. The creation of this book is just one such expression of this belief.

Mom and Dad: You've given me the world and more and provided me with an environment in which I can push myself to my limits. Thank you for never holding me back. Ricky, Emmi, and Joey: I couldn't imagine growing up without all of you by my side. You each inspire me in so many ways.

To the women who graciously offered their time and their life stories for this book, I am indebted to your generosity and vulnerability. Ayanna, Delaney, Gitanjali, Kristin, Martha, Michelle, Natasha, Polina, Raegan, Sarah, and Sunny: You all are unequivocally incredible women and I am honored that your stories have been included in this book. Thank you so very much.

Last, but certainty not least, my beta readers (listed here in alphabetical order by first name):

Abby H., Ali M., Alison G., Allison J., Ally W., Amanda C., Annie B., Annie T., Arze W., Ashlei L., Audrey B., Beth G., Brad H., Bret & Lisa H., Caroline B., Carrie E., Chris S., Christine G., Colleen S., Correen K., Craig T., Daniel K., Dawn C., Deb M., Don L., Emmi E., Eric K., Erica C., Faith N., Farrah F., Gene Z., George K., George V., Grayce M., Grayson R., Greg C., Hannah C., Hannah R., Hatti T., Janelle J., Janet W., Jen H., Jen S., Jena P., Jennifer K., Jennifer S., Jerry and Polly E., Jillian K., Jim F., Joey E, Joey H., Juli H., Karen & Chuck K., Karis S., Kate G., Kate M., Kelly S., Kennia P., Kristi D., Kristin F., Kristin K., Libby S., Linda B., Lisa M., Lisa R., Lisa S., Lisa S., Lori K., Mandy S., Margie B., Maria D., Maryann & Eugene P., Matt E., Mckenzie K., Mehdy S., Melinda U., Michael Z., Morgen & Ricky E., Natalie S., Neil K., Nicole B., Niki P., Nithika B., Pam P., Patricia M., Patricia W., Peggy K., Reagan S., Reshma D., Robert A., Robyn S., Rooney M., Sandra A., Sandra K., Sarah A., Sarah H., Shailendra G., Sheila A., Shelby K., Tatjana M., Tiffany S., Tori H., Tracy R., and Tristana F.

Most of you are my friends, mentors, and advocates. You have all played an instrumental role in the creation of this book and my development as an individual. You have all helped me realize that my life is filled with so many people who will love and support me endlessly. I am beyond grateful for each and every one of you. Thank you.

APPENDIX

INTRODUCTION:

"20 Quotes on Following Your Dreams to Live a Life You've Imagined." *virtuesforlife.com.* https://www.virtuesforlife.com/20-quotes-on-following-your-dreams-to-live-a-life-youve-imagined/.

Ali, Asad. "Regression Analysis." *slideshare.net,* December 22, 2013, https://www.slideshare.net/linashuja/regression-analysis-29424735.

Dream Lens Media. "Courtney Dewaulter." April 2, 2019. Video, 38:52. https://www.youtube.com/watch?v=DQSiygnDm-U.

First Spark Media. "Running for Good" 2018. Video, 1:14:11. https://www.amazon.com/Running-Good-Fiona-Oakes/dp/B07L5PJ728/.

Heagen, Paul. "The Pain of Change Is Not Going To Change Anything." *definingmoments.me,* May 23, 2016, https://definingmoments.me/change/.

"INSPIRING QUOTES BY LAO TZU." *optimize.me.* https://www. optimize.me/quotes/lao-tzu/383026-if-you-do-not-change-direction-you-may-end-up/.

Peterson, Savannah. "How Many Lives Are You, Really?" *designingyour.life,* July 26, 2016, https://designingyour.life/how-many-lives-are-you-really/.

TEDx Talks. "TEDxToronto—Drew Dudley Leading with Lollipops." October 7, 2010. Video, 6:20. https://www.youtube.com/watch?v=hVCBrkrFrBE.

CHAPTER 1:

Albright, Madeleine. "Madeleine Albright: My Undiplomatic Moment." *nytimes.com.* February 12, 2016. https://www.nytimes.com/2016/02/13/opinion/madeleine-albright-my-undiplomatic-moment.html.

Ananthaswamy, Anil and Douglas, Kate. "The origins of sexism: How men came to rule 12,000 years ago." *newscientist.com.* April 18, 2018. https://www.newscientist.com/article/mg23831740-400-the-origins-of-sexism-how-men-came-to-rule-12000-years-ago/.

Anderson, Hans Christian. *The Little Mermaid.* Hans Christian Andersen Centre at the University of Southern Denmark. 2014. https://andersen.sdu.dk/moocfiles/littlemermaid.pdf.

Ang, Katerina. "Why women are meaner to each other than men are to women." *marketwatch.com.* March 5, 2018. https://www.

marketwatch.com/story/why-women-are-meaner-to-each-oth-er-than-men-are-to-women-2018-03-05.

Aspinall, Georgia. "Here Are the Countries Where It's Still Really Difficult for Women to Vote." *graziadaily.co.uk*. June 2, 2018. https://graziadaily.co.uk/life/real-life/countries-where-wom-en-can-t-vote/.

Astier, Marie- Bénédicte. Aphrodite, known as the "Venus de Milo," louvre.fr, https://www.louvre.fr/en/oeuvre-notices/aphrodite-known-venus-de-milo.

Barber, Brad M and Terrance Odean. "BOYS WILL BE BOYS: GENDER, OVERCONFIDENCE, AND COMMON STOCK INVESTMENT." *The Quarterly Journal of Economics*. February 2001. https://faculty.haas.berkeley.edu/odean/papers/gender/BoysWillBeBoys.pdf.

Bryson, Bill. *The Body: A Guide for Participants.* New York: Penguin Random House. 2019.

Cowie, Ashley. "Ancient Laws and Women's Rights: The 6000-Year-Old World War Continues." *ancient-origins.net*. November 12, 2018. https://www.ancient-origins.net/history-ancient-traditions/ancient-laws-0010981.

McCarthy, Chris. "English Riddle: Can you answer the question?" *ecenglish.com*. November 16, 2008. https://www.ecenglish.com/learnenglish/lessons/english-riddle-can-you-answer-question.

Cohen-Zada, Danny, Krumer Alex, Rosenboim Mosi, and Shapir Offer Moshe. "Choking under Pressure and Gender." *Ben-Gu-*

rion *University of the Negev.* September 27, 2016. https://www. researchgate.net/publication/308901292_Choking_Under_ Pressure_and_Gender.

DiFeliciantonia, Samantha. "Alone we can do so little; together we can do so much." – Helen Keller. *teambonding.com.* https:// www.teambonding.com/power-of-communication/.

Dubey, Tanvi. "10 inspirational quotes by Serena Williams that show what it takes to be a champion." *yourstory.com.* September 26, 2019. https://yourstory.com/herstory/2019/09/inspirational-quotes-serena-williams-champion.

Frank, Robert H., Thomas Gilovich and Dennis T. Regan. "Does Studying Economics Inhibit Cooperation?" *The Journal of Economic Perspectives.* Volume 7. Issue 2. (Spring, 1993). 159-171. https://www.gwern.net/docs/economics/1993-frank.pdf.

Gabriel, Allison S., Marcus M. Butts and Michael T. Sliter. "Women Experience More Incivility at Work—Especially from Other Women." *hbr.org.* March 28, 2018. https://hbr.org/2018/03/women-experience-more-incivility-at-work-especially-from-other-women.

"George Byron Quotes." *allauthor.com.* https://allauthor.com/ quotes/105439/

"Greek Creation Myth." *cs.williams.edu.* https://www.cs.williams. edu/~lindsey/myths/myths_16.html.

Kearl, Holly. "Elusive Matriarchy: The Impact of the Native American and Feminist Movements on Navajo Gender Dynamics."

Santa Clara University Undergraduate Journal of History,
Series II. 2006. https://scholarcommons.scu.edu/cgi/viewcon-
tent.cgi?article=1106&context=historical-perspectives.

Mark, Joshua J. "Women in Ancient Egypt." *ancient.eu.* November
4, 2016. https://www.ancient.eu/article/623/women-in-ancient-
egypt/.

Mohan, Pavithra. "Study: Women rank better than men at these
leadership traits." *fastcompany.com.* September 24, 2018.
https://www.fastcompany.com/90240949/study-women-rank-
better-than-men-at-these-leadership-traits.

"Neolithic Times," *slideshare.net.* April 3, 2014. https://www.slide-
share.net/maryamfarooqi/neolithic-times.

"One in ten girls in sub-Saharan Africa miss school during their
period." gemreportunesco.com. April 24, 2018. https://gem-
reportunesco.wordpress.com/2018/04/24/one-in-ten-girls-in-
sub-saharan-africa-miss-school-during-their-period/.

Pocha, Sejal Kapadia. "The 25 greatest female villains in film."
stylist.co.uk. 2014. https://www.stylist.co.uk/life/the-greatest-
female-villains-in-film/55556.

"Report of the APA Task Force on the Sexualization of Girls." *American Psychological Association.* 2007. https://www.apa.org/pi/
women/programs/girls/report-summary.pdf.

"Secretary-General's remarks to General Assembly on Human
Rights Defenders [as delivered]." *un.org.* December 18, 2018.
https://www.un.org/sg/en/content/sg/statement/2018-12-18/sec-

retary-generals-remarks-general-assembly-human-rights-de-
fenders-delivered.

Seale, Natalie. History Quotes. *keepinspiring.me*. https://www.
keepinspiring.me/history-quotes/.

Stankiewicz, Julie M. Rosselli, Francine. "Women as Sex Objects
and Victims in Print Advertisements." *Springer Science +
Business Media*. January 15, 2008. http://citeseerx.ist.psu.edu/
viewdoc/download?doi=10.1.1.465.4923&rep=rep1&type=pdf.

Swift, Jaimee and Hannah Gould. "Not an Object: On Sexualization and Exploitation of Women and Girls." *unicefusa.org*.
January 15, 2020. https://www.unicefusa.org/stories/not-ob-
ject-sexualization-and-exploitation-women-and-girls/30366.

Thorpe, JR. "How Infertility Was Talked About Throughout History—Because to Fight a Taboo, You Need to Understand Its
Origins." *bustle.com*. April 14, 2015. https://www.bustle.com/
articles/76161-how-infertility-was-talked-about-throughout-
history-because-to-fight-a-taboo-you-need-to.

"Timeline of Legal History of Women in the United States."
nationalwomenshistoryalliance.org, https://nationalwomen-
shistoryalliance.org/resources/womens-rights-movement/
detailed-timeline/.

Urban, Tim. "Putting Time in Perspective—UPDATED." *wait-
butwhy.com*. August 22, 2013. https://waitbutwhy.com/2013/08/
putting-time-in-perspective.html.

Schopenhauer, Arthur. THE ESSAYS OF ARTHUR SCHOPEN-HAUER. gutenberg.org. January 18, 2004. https://www.gutenberg.org/files/10739/10739-h/10739-h.htm.

Zenger, Jack and Joseph Folkman. "Research: Women Score Higher Than Men in Most Leadership Skills." *hbr.org*. June 25, 2019. https://hbr.org/2019/06/research-women-score-higher-than-men-in-most-leadership-skills.

Zerzan, John. "Patriarchy, Civilization, and the Origins of Gender." *theanarchistlibrary.org*. April 13, 2010. https://the-anarchistlibrary.org/library/john-zerzan-patriarchy-civilization-and-the-origins-of-gender.

CHAPTER 2:

"Before anything else, preparation is the key to success." *quotes.net*. https://www.quotes.net/quote/40397.

Bruce, Jan. "Sheryl Sandberg's Guide to Grief, Growth and Getting It Right in Today's Business Climate." *Forbes.com*. August 25, 2017. https://www.forbes.com/sites/janbruce/2017/08/25/sheryl-sandbergs-guide-to-grief-growth-and-getting-it-right-in-todays-business-climate/#67534d881834.

de Vries, Manfred F.R. Kets. "Are You a Victim of Victim Syndrome?" *INSEAD*. 2012. https://sites.insead.edu/facultyresearch/research/doc.cfm?did=50114.

"Dr Brené Brown: Empathy vs Sympathy." twentyonetoys. com. https://twentyonetoys.com/blogs/teaching-empathy/brene-brown-empathy-vs-sympathy.

"Purposeful Quotes." *jarofquotes.com*. https://www.jarofquotes. com/view.php?tag=purposeful.

TEDx Talks. "BUILDING EMPATHY: How to hack empathy and get others to care more | Jamil Zaki | TEDxMarin." October 18, 2017. Video, 13:18. https://www.youtube.com/watch?v=-DspKSYxYDM.

CHAPTER 3:

Anthony, Sebastian. "Harvard & MIT create first self-assembling robots—the first real Transformers." *extremetech.com*. August 8, 2014. https://www.extremetech.com/extreme/187736-har-vard-mit-create-first-self-assembling-robots-the-first-real-transformers.

Barker, Eric. "A Navy SEAL explains 8 secrets to grit and resilience." *theladders.com*. June 5, 2019. https://www.theladders. com/career-advice/a-navy-seal-explains-8-secrets-to-grit-and-resilience.

"Challenge Participants." *youngscientistlab.com*. https://www. youngscientistlab.com/challenge.

Denchak, Melissa, "Flint Water Crisis: Everything You Need to Know." *nrdc.org*. November 8, 2018. https://www.nrdc.org/sto-ries/flint-water-crisis-everything-you-need-know.

Dialynus, E.G. and A.N. Angelakis. "The Evolution of Water Supply Technologies in Ancient Crete, Greece." *worldwatermuseum. com*. http://worldwatermuseum.com/the-evolution-of-water-supply-technologies-in-ancient-crete-greece/.

Duckworth, Angela. *Grit: The Power of Passion and Perseverance.* New York: Scribner, 2016.

Dweck, Carol. "What Having a 'Growth Mindset' Actually Means." *hbr.org.* January 13, 2016. https://hbr.org/2016/01/what-having-a-growth-mindset-actually-means.

Hilmantel, Robin. "4 Signs You Have Grit." *time.com.* May 12, 2016. https://time.com/4327035/4-signs-you-have-grit/.

Hilmantel, Robin. "4 Signs You Have Grit." *time.com.* May 12, 2016. https://time.com/4327035/4-signs-you-have-grit/.

Khine, Dr. Michelle. Scientist and Dr. Michelle Khine: "Growing Up, Nobody Thought I Was Smart." *forbes.com.* March 22, 2018. https://www.forbes.com/sites/sallypercy/2018/03/22/scientist-and-innovator-dr-michelle-khine-growing-up-nobody-thought-i-was-smart/#1683dce264ee.

"Lead poisoning and health." *who.int.* August 23, 2019. https://www.who.int/news-room/fact-sheets/detail/lead-poisoning-and-health.

"Marie Curie Forbes Quotes." *forbes.com.* https://www.forbes.com/quotes/6520/.

"Marie Curie (1867 – 1934)." *bbc.co.uk.* http://www.bbc.co.uk/history/historic_figures/curie_marie.shtml.

Matheson, Rob. "Wireless, wearable toxic-gas detector." *news.mit.edu.* June 20, 2016. http://news.mit.edu/2016/wireless-wearable-toxic-gas-detector-0630.

May, Jake. "Still standing: Flint residents tell their stories about living with poisoned water." *mlive.com*. https://www.mlive.com/news/page/still_standing_flint_residents.html.

"Martin Luther King Jr." *wisdomtoinspire.com*. https://wisdomtoinspire.com/t/martin-luther-king-jr/4ke9wU2P/if-you-cant-fly-then-run.

Meah, Asad. "35 Inspirational Marie Curie Quotes on Success." *awakenthegreatnesswithin.com*. https://www.awakenthegreatnesswithin.com/35-inspirational-marie-curie-quotes-on-success/.

Movieclips. "Apollo 13 (1995)—Failure Is Not an Option Scene (6/11) | Movieclips." August 3, 2017. Video, 2:09. https://www.youtube.com/watch?v=Tid44iy6Rjs.

Rowe. Aaron. "Hack: Young Professor Makes Lab-on-a-Chip with Shrinky Dink and Toaster Oven." *wired.com*. December 4, 2007. https://www.wired.com/2007/12/macgyver-scienc/.

Sener, Saffron. "Shrinky Dinks: A Love Story." *baremagazine.org*. October 3, 2018. http://www.baremagazine.org/shrinky-dinks-love-story

"TETHYS." *theoi.com*. https://www.theoi.com/Titan/TitanisTethys.html.

"Vintage Shrinky Dinks: How these crafty toys were invented & how they work." *clickamericana.com*. https://clickamericana.com/toys-and-games/vintage-shrinky-dinks.

CHAPTER 4:

"Arnold J. Toynbee Quotes." *All Author.* https://allauthor.com/quotes/54852/.

Chouinard, Michelle M. *Children's Questions.* Wiley-Blackwell. 2007 https://www.wiley.com/en-us/Children's+Questions-p-9781405176330.

Coyle, Daniel. *The Culture Code: The Secrets of Highly Successful Groups.* New York. Bantam Books. 2018.

Covey, Stephen R. *The 7 Habit of Highly Effective People.* Simon & Schuster Paperbacks. 1989.

"Eric Ries: 'Figuring out how to ask.'" A More Beautiful Question. https://amorebeautifulquestion.com/figuring-out-how-to-ask/.

Detert, James R. and Ethan R. Burris. "Can Your Employees Really Speak Freely?" *hbr.org.* https://hbr.org/2016/01/can-your-employees-really-speak-freely

Grandhi, Rama and Satya Diwake. "The art and science of asking questions is the source of all knowledge!" *Medium.* March 4, 2018. https://medium.com/@diwakargrandhi/the-art-and-science-of-asking-questions-is-the-source-of-all-knowledge-b49144e2479c.

Loewenstein, George. "The Psychology of Curiosity: A Review and Reinterpretation." *American Psychological Association Psychological Bulletin,* vol. 116, 1994. Accessed September 17, 2019. http://www.andrew.cmu.edu/user/gl20/GeorgeLoewenstein/Papers_files/pdf/PsychofCuriosity.pdf.

Molokhia, Dalia. "The Importance Of Being Curious." *Harvard Business Publishing*. May 24, 2018. https://www.harvardbusiness.org/the-importance-of-being-curious/.

Neyfakh, Leon. "Are we asking the right questions?" *Boston Globe*. May 20, 2012. https://www.bostonglobe.com/ideas/2012/05/19/just-ask/k9PATXFdpL6ZmkreSiRYGP/story.html

"Observing the journals of Leonardo da Vinci." *Journaling Habit*. March 25, 2017. https://journalinghabit.com/observing-journals-leonardo-da-vinci/.

Oleson, T.J. "BJARNI, HERJÓLFSSON." *Dictionary of Canadian Biography*, vol. 1. University of Toronto/Université Laval, 2003. Accessed September 3, 2019. http://www.biographi.ca/en/bio/bjarni_herjolfsson_1E.html.

"Polynesian History and Origin." PBS. accessed September 3, 2019. https://www.pbs.org/wayfinders/polynesian2.html.

"Polynesian Wayfinders." Solar Dynamics Observatory. Video, April 10, 2012. https://www.youtube.com/watch?v=r4EooiQcuyE.

Raffaele, Paul. "Speaking Bonobo." *Smithsonian Magazine*. November 2006. https://www.smithsonianmag.com/science-nature/speaking-bonobo-134931541/.

Rana, Zat, "The Underutilized Power of Questions." *Medium*. November 23, 2017. https://medium.com/personal-growth/the-underutilized-power-of-questions-how-einstein-and-da-vinci-found-genius-d7ef7d99f7bd.

"SHORT ON CURIOSITY: THE STORY OF BJARNI JERJOLFS-SON." Ultimate History Project. Accessed September 3, 2019. http://ultimatehistoryproject.com/short-on-curiosity.html.

Sierzputowski, Kate. "Recently Digitized Journals Grant Visitors Access to Leonardo da Vinci's Detailed Engineering Schematics and Musings." *COLOSSAL.* September 5, 2018. https://www.thisiscolossal.com/2018/09/recently-digitized-journals-by-leonardo-da-vinci/.

TED. "Why we have too few women leaders | Sheryl Sandberg." December 21, 2010. Video, https://www.youtube.com/watch?reload=9&v=18uDutylDa4.

Zöllner, Frank. "Leonardo da Vinci, 1452–1519: the complete paintings and drawings." Collins Library Archives. 2003. Accessed September 20, 2019. https://alliance-primo.hosted.exlibrisgroup.com/primo-explore/fulldisplay?docid=CP71127511200001451&context=L&vid=UPUGS&lang=en_US.

CHAPTER 5:

"30 of Our Favorite Quotes On Innovation." *workspace.digital.* http://workspace.digital/30-favorite-quotes-innovation/.

Alper, Tim. "Talmud-inspired learning craze sweeps South Korea." *Jewish Telegraphic Agency.* January 14, 2019. https://www.jta.org/2019/01/14/global/talmud-inspired-learning-craze-sweeps-south-korea.

"Ayanna MacCalla Howard." *Georgia Tech School of Electrical and Computer Engineering Faculty Staff Directory.* https://www.ece.gatech.edu/faculty-staff-directory/ayanna-maccalla-howard.

Bouygues, Helen Lee. "3 Simple Habits to Improve Your Critical Thinking," *Harvard Business Review.* May 6, 2019. https://hbr.org/2019/05/3-simple-habits-to-improve-your-critical-thinking.

Howard, Ayanna. "Why We Need to Build Robots We Can Trust." *TED.* November 2018. https://www.ted.com/talks/ayanna_howard_why_we_need_to_build_robots_we_can_trust.

"Innovation is the ability to see change as an opportunity—not a threat." *azquotes.com,* https://www.azquotes.com/quote/1059252.

Meah, Asad. "35 Inspirational Michael Dell Quotes on Success." *Awakening the Greatness Within.* https://www.awakenthegreatnesswithin.com/35-inspirational-michael-dell-quotes-on-success/.

"Sandy Lerner Biography," *Encyclopedia of World Biography,* https://www.notablebiographies.com/newsmakers2/2005-La-Pr/Lerner-Sandy.html.

Scriven PhD, Olivia A. "Why So Few? African American Women in STEM—Part II: By the Numbers." *Scientista.* May 7, 2013. http://www.scientistafoundation.com/scientista-spotlights/why-so-few-african-american-women-in-stem-part-ii-by-the-numbers.

Rizzo, Meredith. "Being Different Helped A NASA Roboticist Achieve Her Dream." *NPR.* December 19, 2017. https://www.npr.org/2017/12/19/569474169/being-different-helped-a-nasa-roboticist-achieve-her-dream.

"20 Wise, Humbling Quotes from a Nobel Prize Winning Psychologist." *Inc.* January 21, 2016. https://www.inc.com/sims-wyeth/20-wise-humbling-quotes-from-a-nobel-prize-winning-psychologist.html.

CHAPTER 6:

Agyei, Steve. "It is hard to fail, but it is worse never to have tried to succeed." *medium.com.* December 17, 2015. https://medium.com/@steveagyeibeyondlifestyle/it-is-hard-to-fail-but-it-is-worse-never-to-have-tried-to-succeed-180982176a09.

Brody, Jane E. "The Worst That Could Happen? Going Blind, People Say." February 20, 2015. *nytimes.com.* https://www.nytimes.com/2017/02/20/well/the-worst-that-could-happen-going-blind-people-say.html.

Cherry, Kendra. "Quotes from Albert Bandura on His Theories." *verywellmind.com.* May 5, 2020. https://www.verywellmind.com/albert-bandura-quotes-2795687.

Dalla-Camina, Megan. "Are You Playing to Your Strengths at Work?" *Psychology Today* November 11, 2018. https://www.psychologytoday.com/us/blog/real-women/201811/are-you-playing-your-strengths-work.

Duxbury, Christen. "It Is Not the Critic Who Counts." *Theodore Roosevelt Conservation Partnership*. January 18, 2011. https://www.trcp.org/2011/01/18/it-is-not-the-critic-who-counts/.

Gorlinski, Virginia. "Pygmalion." *Encyclopedia Britannica*. https://www.britannica.com/topic/Pygmalion.

"High achievement always takes place in the framework of high expectation." *statusmind.com*. http://statusmind.com/smart-quotes-2894/.

Lambe, Stacy. "*Space Jam* 20 Years Later: How 'I Believe I Can Fly' Transformed R. Kelly's Career." *etonline.com*. November 15, 2016. https://www.etonline.com/features/202857_.

Nobel, Carmen. "The Power of Rituals in Life, Death, and Business." *Harvard Business School*. June 3, 2013. https://hbswk.hbs.edu/item/the-power-of-rituals-in-life-death-and-business.

Simstrom, Liana. "WATCH: Can You Affect Another Person's Behavior with Your Thoughts?" *NPR*. September 7, 2018. https://www.npr.org/sections/health-shots/2018/09/07/644530036/watch-can-you-affect-another-persons-behavior-with-your-thoughts.

"Top 20 Serena Williams Quotes to Inspire You to Rise Up and Win." *Goalcast*. August 8, 2017. https://www.goalcast.com/2017/08/08/top-20-serena-williams-quotes-to-inspire-you-to-rise-up-win/.

"World Report on Disability." *World Health Organization*. 2011. https://www.who.int/disabilities/world_report/2011/accessible_en.pdf.

CHAPTER 7:

"Altruistic babies? Infants are willing to give up food, help others." *ScienceDaily*. February 4, 2020. https://www.sciencedaily.com/releases/2020/02/200204091354.htm.

"Bengal famine inspired love for the poor." *The Irish Times*. September 8, 1997. https://www.irishtimes.com/news/bengal-famine-inspired-love-for-the-poor-1.104082.

Bryson, Bill. "Why the most awe-inspiring wonder in the universe is inside your head." *Daily Mail*. September 7, 2019. https://www.dailymail.co.uk/health/article-7438997/Bill-Bryson-returns-captivating-journey-mysteries-human-body.html.

Emmons, Robert. "The Benefits of Gratitude," *Greater Good Magazine*, November 2010, https://greatergood.berkeley.edu/video/item/the_benefits_of_gratitude.

Gina, Francesca and Maryam Kouchaki. "We behave a lot more badly than we remember." *The Conversation*. June 7, 2016. https://theconversation.com/we-behave-a-lot-more-badly-than-we-remember-59727.

"Giving thanks can make you happier." *Harvard Health Publishing*. https://www.health.harvard.edu/healthbeat/giving-thanks-can-make-you-happier.

Grant, Adam. "In the Company of Givers and Takers." *Harvard Business Review*. April 2013. https://hbr.org/2013/04/in-the-company-of-givers-and-takers.

"Gratitude." *Online Etymology Dictionary.* https://www.etymonline. com/word/gratitude.

"Gratitude Lounge." *Gratefulness.org.*

"Helping others is the way we help ourselves. – Oprah Winfrey." quotemaster.org. https://www.quotemaster.org/q3a2ce245cb-f35375b0b0ed4a43522074.

Kosloski, Philip. "7 Saintly quotes about being thankful." *Aleteia.* November 19 2017. https://aleteia.org/2017/11/19/7-saintly-quotes-about-being-thankful/.

Kraut, Richard. *The Quality of Life: Aristotle Revised.* Oxford University Press. 2018.

Lewis, Jone Johnson. "Mother Teresa Quotes." *ThoughtCo.* June 14, 2017., https://www.thoughtco.com/mother-teresa-quotes-3530149.

"Mother Teresa Biography." *Biography.com.* April 27, 2017. https://www.biography.com/religious-figure/mother-teresa.

Mukhopadhyay, Sougata. "Kolkata and the Inevitability of Mother Teresa." *News 18 India.* September 4, 2016. https://www.news18.com/news/india/kolkata-and-the-inevitability-of-mother-teresa-1289048.html.

Roy, Tirthankar. "The Bengal Famine of 1943." *History Today Volume 69.* July 7, 2019. https://www.historytoday.com/archive/feature/bengal-famine-1943.

Sealy, Raegan. "How rap saves lives." TED video. https://www.youtube.com/watch?v=Lfde98ZHKVQ.

Sullivan, Meg. "Your brain might be hard-wired for altruism." *UCLA Newsroom*. March 18, 2016. http://newsroom.ucla.edu/releases/your-brain-might-be-hard-wired-for-altruism.

The Creative Brain, 2019, Netflix, https://www.netflix.com/title/81090128.

Zehra Rosheena, "Direct Action Day: When Massive Communal Riots Made Kolkata Bleed." *The Quint*. August, 24, 2016. https://www.thequint.com/news/india/direct-action-day-when-massive-communal-riots-made-kolkata-bleed.

CHAPTER 8:

"Accomplishments will prove to be a journey, not a destination." *passiton.com.* https://www.passiton.com/inspirational-quotes/6715-accomplishments-will-prove-to-be-a-journey-not.

Ackerman, Courtney E. "What is Kaplan's Attention Restoration Theory (ART)?" *PostivePsychology.com.* October 7, 2019. https://positivepsychology.com/attention-restoration-theory/.

Ashworth, Hannah. "How long is your DNA?" *Science Focus.* https://www.sciencefocus.com/the-human-body/how-long-is-your-dna/.

Blackburn, Simon. "Meet the Flintstones." *The New Republic.* November 25, 2002. https://newrepublic.com/article/66598/meet-the-flintstones.

Chism, Marlene. "The Greatest Agent for Change." *Marlenechism. com.* January 22, 2015. https://marlenechism.com/blog/the-greatest-agent-for-change/.

Cromwell, Casey. "How 7 Inspirational Women Define Success." *entitymag.com.* December 9, 2017. https://www.entitymag. com/7-inspirational-women-define-success/.

"Genes, Evolution, and Environment." *Vancouver Community College Learning Centre.* 2016. https://library.vcc.ca/learningcen-tre//pdf/vcclc/Psychology%20-%20Genes%20and%20the%20 Environment.pdf.

Heller, Seth. "Sunny Stroeer Is the Fastest Woman You've Never Heard Of." *Outside.* February 1, 2017. https://www.outsideon-line.com/2153796/sunny-stroeer-sets-speed-record-aconcagua.

Juma, Norbert. "Florence Nightingale quotes on Life, Communication and Nursing." *everydaypower.com.* May 5, 2019. https:// everydaypower.com/florence-nightingale-quotes/.

Meah, Asad. "50 Inspirational Oprah Winfrey Quotes on Success." *awakenthegreatnesswithin.com.* https://www. awakenthegreatnesswithin.com/50-inspirational-oprah-win-frey-quotes-on-success/.

Meah, Asad. "50 Motivational Eric Thomas Quotes to Unleash Your Greatness." awakenthegreatnesswithin.com. https://www. awakenthegreatnesswithin.com/50-motivational-eric-thom-as-quotes-to-unleash-your-greatness/.

Moore, Catherine. "What is Eudaimonia? Aristotle and Eudaimonic Well-Being." *PostivePsychology.com*. November 2, 2020. https://positivepsychology.com/eudaimonia/.

"Our Story," *AWExpedition.org*. https://www.awexpeditions.org/about.

Prokorenko, Kat. "How to Quit Talking and Begin Doing." *Medium.com*. December 20, 2017. https://medium.com/future-of-work/how-to-quit-talking-and-begin-doing-a46c406cde3f.

"Social Comparison Theory." *Psychology Today*. https://www.psychologytoday.com/us/basics/social-comparison-theory.

CHAPTER 9:

"6 Powerful Benefits of Vulnerability and Shame—Yes, you read that right." *intentioninspired.com*. https://intentioninspired.com/6-powerful-benefits-of-vulnerability-and-shame/.

Aurelius, Marcus. *Meditations*. New York: The Modern Library. http://seinfeld.co/library/meditations.pdf.

Belote, Thom. "Facing Vulnerability." *questformeaning.org*. https://www.questformeaning.org/spiritual-themes/facing-vulnerability/.

"Brené Brown Inspired One Young Man to Say, 'I Love You.'" *Oprah Winfrey Network*. September 22, 2013. https://www.youtube.com/watch?v=bonFfqAoF_c.

Caddell, Jenev. "Understanding the Stigma Around Mental Illness." *verywellmind.com*. June 21, 2019. https://www.verywellmind.com/mental-illness-and-stigma-2337677.

"Excerpt from Brené Brown's *Rising Strong*: The Physics of Vulnerability." *parade.com*. September 4, 2015. https://parade.com/420360/parade/excerpt-from-brene-browns-rising-strong-the-physics-of-vulnerability/.

McLeod, Saul. "Erik Erikson's Stages of Psychosocial Development." *simplypsychology.org*. 2018. https://www.simplypsychology.org/Erik-Erikson.html.

Ovid. "The Metamorphoses." *poetryintranslation.com*. 2000. https://www.poetryintranslation.com/klineasovid.php.

"People are lonely because they build walls instead of bridges.", *forbesquotes.com*. https://www.forbes.com/quotes/5651/.

Schneider, Jacquelyn. "The capability/vulnerability paradox and military revolutions: Implications for computing, cyber, and the onset of war." *Journal of Strategic Studies*. August 22, 2019. https://www.tandfonline.com/doi/full/10.1080/01402390.2019.1627209.

Seppälä, Emma. "What Bosses Gain by Being Vulnerable." *Harvard Business Review*. December 11, 2014. https://hbr.org/2014/12/what-bosses-gain-by-being-vulnerable.

"The Adult Chair Model." theadultchair.com. https://theadultchair.com/adult-chair-model/.

"The Aeneid, Book IV." sparknotes.com. https://www.sparknotes.com/lit/aeneid/section4/.

The Vulnerability Challenge. https://thevulnerabilitychallenge.com/.

Virgil. "The Aeneid." *poetryintranslation.com.* 2002. http://people.virginia.edu/~jdk3t/AeneidTrKline2002.pdf.

"Vulnerable." merriam-webster.com. https://www.merriam-webster.com/dictionary/vulnerable.

"Vulnerability Management Life Cycle." *Centers for Disease Control and Prevention.* https://www.cdc.gov/cancer/npcr/tools/security/vmlc.htm.

"Vulnerability vs. Over-sharing: Where to Draw the Line?" *becomingwhoyouare.net.* https://www.becomingwhoyouare.net/blog/vulnerability-vs-over-sharing-where-to-draw-the-line.

CHAPTER 10:

Becker-Phelps, Leslie. "Don't Just React: Choose Your Response." *psychologytoday.com.* July 23, 2013. https://www.psychologytoday.com/us/blog/making-change/201307/dont-just-react-choose-your-response.

Carli, Julie. "Remembrance for Walter Mischel, Psychologist Who Devised the Marshmallow Test." *npr.org.* September 21, 2018. https://www.npr.org/sections/health-shots/2018/09/21/650015068/remembrance-for-walter-mischel-psychologist-who-devised-the-marshmallow-test.

"Closer than ever: It is 100 seconds to midnight." *thebulletin.org.*
https://thebulletin.org/doomsday-clock/current-time/?fb-
clid=IwAR2QNehANcmKpiAyasWo3imFKBnpTvvT-eoYm-
Jb8crXRNiiLH-C1Sg6toog.

Cuncic, Arlin. "An Overview of Viktor Frankl's Logotherapy." very-
wellmind.com. October 6, 2019. https://www.verywellmind.
com/an-overview-of-victor-frankl-s-logotherapy-4159308.

"Dylan Thomas." *poets.org.* https://poets.org/poet/dylan-thomas.

Haywood, Jackie. "The Dance of Change." *illuminateyou.co.uk.*
August 30, 2019. https://www.illuminateyou.co.uk/blog/the-
dance-of-change.

Hyatt, Michael. "How a Small Shift in Your Vocabulary Can
Instantly Change Your Attitude." *michaelhyatt.com.* https://
michaelhyatt.com/how-a-shift-in-your-vocabulary-can-in-
stantly-change-your-attitude/.

"Manhattan Project." *history.com.* July 26, 2017. https://www.history.
com/topics/world-war-ii/the-manhattan-project.

Mark, Joshua J. "Heraclitus of Ephesus." *ancient.eu.* July 14, 2010.
https://www.ancient.eu/Heraclitus_of_Ephesos/.

Morrison, Ryan. "Doomsday clock moves the closest to midnight
in its 73-year history." *dailymail.co.uk.* January 23, 2020. https://
www.dailymail.co.uk/sciencetech/article-7921447/Doomsday-
clock-moves-forward-20-seconds-bringing-apocalypse-closer-
before.html.

Mehta, Viral. "The Last of the Human Freedoms." *huffpost.com.* January 3, 2013, https://www.huffpost.com/entry/life-choices_b_2390373.

Nolen, Jeannette L. "Walter Mischel." *britannica.com.* https://www.britannica.com/biography/Walter-Mischel.

Neutrinos and Other Matters: Selected Works of Frederick Reines. New Jersey: World Scientific Publishing Co.

"Power of Words." *fropky.com.* https://www.fropky.com/power-words-vt20348.html.

"The Trinity Test." *history.com.* April 23, 2010. https://www.history.com/topics/world-war-ii/trinity-test.

"Viktor Frankl (1905-1997)." *goodtherapy.org.* https://www.goodtherapy.org/famous-psychologists/viktor-frankl.html.

Welna, David. "The End May Be Nearer: Doomsday Clock Moves Within 100 Seconds of Midnight." *npr.org.* January 23, 2020. https://www.npr.org/2020/01/23/799047659/the-end-may-be-nearer-doomsday-clock-moves-within-100-seconds-of-midnight.

Yardley, William. "Martyl Langsdorf, Doomsday Clock Designer, Dies at 96." *nytimes.com.* April 10, 2013. https://www.nytimes.com/2013/04/11/us/martyl-langsdorf-artist-behind-doomsday-clock-dies-at-96.html

Made in the USA
Monee, IL
12 August 2020

37330961R00144